DIALECTICS

DIALECTICS

A Controversy-Oriented Approach to the Theory of Knowledge

Nicholas Rescher

State University of New York Press · Albany · 1977

First published in 1977 by
State University of New York Press
Albany, New York 12246

Made and printed in the United States of America

Library of Congress Cataloging in Publication Data

Rescher, Nicholas.
Dialectics.

Includes bibliographical references and indexes.
1. Dialectic—Addresses, essays, lectures.
2. Knowledge, Theory of—Addresses, essays, lectures.
I. Title.
B105.D48R47   121   77-9542
ISBN 0-87395-372-X

For Six Dialectical Thinkers

Mortimer Adler
Anthony Kenny
Paul Lorenzen
Arne Naess
Ch. Perelman
Stephen Toulmin

Contents

Preface

This little book explores a disputational approach to inquiry. Its origin lies in the scepticism chapter of my *Methodological Pragmatism* (Oxford: Basil Blackwell, 1977), which poses the prospect of utilizing disputation and rational controversy as a model for issues in the theory of knowledge. This connection indicates the setting of the present deliberations as part of a larger effort to exhibit the philosophical utility of a fusion of Hegelian and pragmatic ideas. (To be sure, the book's concern with dialectics is largely oriented towards the older, rhetorical tradition and does not represent an attempt to interpret the specific dialectical mechanisms of Hegel's philosophy.)

The term *dialectic* is used here to denote the discipline itself, the term *dialectics* to denote the process of engaging in the discipline—the practice or use of it.

The materials presented here were initially offered as a public-lecture series at the University of Pittsburgh during the winter term of 1976 and concurrently presented as lectures for graduate students at the University of Western Ontario. The discussions occasioned by these lectures were helpful in refining the presentation.

Parts of the book were written in the course of an academic visit in Oxford during the Michaelmas term of 1975. This visit was aided by a grant-in-aid from the American Council of Learned Societies in support of research on the epistemology of the idealist tradition. I acknowledge this assistance with gratitude. And I am also grateful to Corpus Christi College for affording me an academic home during this visit in Oxford.

I am indebted to Barbara Hill, Cynthia Freeland, Timo Airaksinen, and an anonymous publisher's reader for reading the manuscript and offering some useful suggestions for its improvement. Kathleen Reznik deserves my grateful thanks for preparing the typescript through a succession of revisions.
Pittsburgh
April 1976

Introduction

Dialectic is, as it were, the *alchemy* of philosophy. It is all things to all men: to some, the most rigorous procedure for exact and cogent thinking; to others, a way of getting outside the established rules—an "anything goes" process for breaking through to unfettered innovations of thinking. For some it is the quintessential method of inquiring thought, for others the quintessential antimethod.[1]

Since the days when Hegel reestablished dialectic as a central theme of modern philosophy, various schools of thought have viewed this discipline in very different ways: as part of the causal pattern of historical development (the Marxists), as a branch of philosophical ontology (contemporary German neo-Hegelianism), as a sector of rhetorical tradition (the "New Rhetoric" of Chaim Perelman and his associates), and as a way of systematizing the testing process for scientific theories (Karl Popper and his school).[2] The present study of dialectics has kinship with the last two of these approaches. Its starting point lies squarely in the rhetorical tradition whose fountainhead is Aristotle. In the sense of "dialectics" at issue here, Plato is the grandfather but Aristotle is the father of the enterprise, and his *Topics* is the pioneer work.[3] However, the ideas of Hegel and his school also make themselves felt, particularly as regards the role of dialectic in the authentication of claims to knowledge.[4]

---

1. Kenneth Burke in *A Grammar of Motives* (published together with *A Rhetoric of Motives* [Cleveland and New York, 1962; Meridian paperback], pp. 403 ff) inventories the bewildering variety of meanings the word "dialectic" has been asked to bear.

2. For (essentially) this taxonomy of dialectical theorizing, and for reference to the literature, see Hans Friedrich Fulda, "Unzulängliche Bemerkungen zur Dialektik" in R. Heede and J. Richter (eds.), *Hegel-Bilanz* (Frankfurt am Main, 1973).

3. For the historical stagesetting, see James Hogan, "The Dialectics of Aristotle," *Philosophical Studies* (Maynooth), 5 (1955): 3–21; and for the early, pre-Aristotelian history of dialectics, see Gilbert Ryle, "The Academy and Dialectic" (= Chapter 5) in his *Collected Essays* (London, 1971), as well as "Dialectic in the Academy" (= Chapter 6), *ibid.* See also J. D. G. Evans, *Aristotle's Concept of Dialectic* (Cambridge, 1977) and G. E. L. Owen (ed.), *Aristotle on Dialectic* (Oxford, 1968).

4. The present discussion leaves wholly out of account the vast body of philosophical discussion of *aporia* or paralogisms—inaugurated by Zeno, enlarged by Plato's Parmenides, painstakingly cultivated by the medievals, and revivified by Kant. This is not due to the (blatantly wrong) impression that this theme is without inherent interest and value—quite the reverse!—

The aim of the present discussion is to explore the philosophical promise of dialectic, or rather one particular version of dialectic—that of disputation, debate, and rational controversy. To get a firm grip on this protean idea, it seems advantageous for present purposes to begin with a very definite (and thus *manageable*) sector of "dialectical" processes, and formal disputation has accordingly been selected as a focus. We shall explore this particular sector of dialectics to see what epistemological lessons can be drawn from it in order to exhibit the utility of such "dialectics" for the theory of knowledge. The goal of this exploration is the development of a dialectical model for the rationalization of cognitive methodology—scientific inquiry specifically included.

Why this focus on disputation? For one principal reason: because *it exhibits epistemological processes at work in a setting of socially conditioned interactions.* This socially oriented perspective is surely a step in the right direction. For the dialectical approach to epistemology is motivated by an anti-Cartesian animus. It deplores the baneful influence of the egocentric orientation of modern epistemology. The traditional and orthodox emphasis on the issues *How can I convince myself? How can I be certain?* invites us to forget the social nature of the ground rules of probative reasoning—their rooting in the issue of: *How can we go about convincing one another?* The dialectics of disputation and controversy provides a useful antidote to such cognitive egocentrism. It insists that we do not forget the buildup of knowledge as a communal enterprise subject to communal standards.

Moreover, since a (presumptively) *rational* community is at issue, the theme of dialectical process will have to be continuous with that of probative propriety. With the breakdown of the medieval synthesis a division arose between rhetoric and logic which by the nineteenth century had become a veritable gulf. Logic went on from strength to strength; rhetoric remained neglected and underdeveloped. But this is unfortunate, since rhetoric embraces not only the study of persuasion but also that of cogent demonstration. On the present perspective, at

but rather simply because it does not lie sufficiently close to the direction of the present concerns. The reader interested in a brief account of this range of issues is referred to the long article "Dialektik" in J. Ritter (ed.), *Historisches Wörterbuch der Philosophie,* vol. 2 (Basel and Stuttgart, 1972), pp. 163–226.

any rate, dialectics is not so much a vehicle for effective persuasion as for reasonable argumentation. In large measure dialectic is to our *factual* knowledge what logic is to our *formal* knowledge: a mechanism of rational validation.

Accordingly, the prime aims of the present discussion are to exhibit the sociocommunal roots of the foundations of rationality, to provide an instrument for the critique of the scepticism implicit in the cognitive solipsism of the Cartesian approach, and to illuminate the communal and controversy-oriented aspects of rational argumentation and inquiry—*scientific* inquiry in particular. This last point is especially important. For the discussion endeavors to develop a version of "dialectics" that does not put the dialectical enterprise into opposition with science, but sees the dialectical and the scientific approaches to rationality as mutually complementary aspects of one and the same cognitive effort.

Our discussion will thus focus upon disputation as a probative mechanism in the *factual* domain. This stance, however, implies no judgment that the disputational model has no utility outside this sphere. Quite to the contrary, several recent writers have endeavored—with considerable success—to develop disputationally inspired mechanisms of strictly logical demonstration.[5] But the issues on the formal and on the factual side are sufficiently distinct that a profitable division of labor can be effected with reference to these boundaries.

Perhaps no recent writer has supported the importance of dialectic and open discussion as an instrumentality in the pursuit of truth more eloquently than John Stuart Mill. His essay *On Liberty* is a prose poem in praise of rational controversy, in which Mill holds dialectic to be a perennial necessity of the rational enterprise, notwithstanding its somewhat negative aspect as an instrument of criticism:

> It is the fashion of the present time to disparage negative logic—that which points out weaknesses in theory or errors in practice, without establishing positive truths. Such negative criticism would indeed be poor enough as an ultimate result; but as a means to attaining any posi-

5. Reference should be made in particular to the work of Paul Lorenzen and his associates. A good exposition is given in Paul Lorenzen and Oswald Schwemmer, *Konstruktive Logik, Ethik und Wissenschaftstheorie*, 2nd ed. (Mannheim, 1975). Cf. also Appendix 2 to Chapter Four below.

tive knowledge or conviction worthy the name, it cannot be valued too highly; and until people are again systematically trained to it, there will be few great thinkers, and a low general average of intellect, in any but the mathematical and physical departments of speculation.[6]

The present discussion seeks to explain and substantiate such a view of the utility of dialectic as an instrument of inquiry.

6. John Stuart Mill, *On Liberty*, ed. A. Castell (New York, 1947), pp. 44–45.

1 The disputational background of dialectic: the structure of formal disputation

1. Formal disputation

Perhaps the clearest, and surely historically the most prominent, instance of dialectical process is formal disputation. Formal disputation is a method for conducting controversial discussions, with one contender defending a thesis in the face of objects and counterarguments made by an adversary. This was a commonplace procedure in universities in the Middle Ages. It served as one of the major training and examining devices in all four faculties of academic instruction: in arts, medicine, and theology, as well as in law. The procedure of disputation before a master and an audience was closely akin to a legal trial in structure and in setting (the *aula* was set up much as a courtroom). It was presided over by a "determiner," the supervising *magister*, who also "determined" it—that is, summarized its result and ruled on the issue under dispute (*quaestio disputata*), exactly as a judge did in a law court.[1] The disputant was faced by a specifically appointed respon-

[1]. A rather romanticized view of the basic set-up can be seen in the famous fresco "The Dispute of St. Thomas Aquinas with the Heretics" in the Church of Santa Maria sopra Minerva in Rome. It is particularly interesting that the foreground is littered with the books used by the disputants as sources for their proof-texts.

dent (*respondens*), who, like a defending attorney, attempted to rebut his points in reply (*respondere de quaestione*).[2]

There had to be general rules for assigning responsibility for the conduct of argumentation and for allocating the "burden of proof" between proponent (*proponens*) and opposing respondent (*respondens, oppenens,* or *quaerens*). These too were taken over bodily from the procedure of the Roman law courts. In particular, it was a cardinal rule that throughout the dialectical process of contention and response, the burden of proof lay with the assertor (*ei qui dicit non ei qui negat*). Disputation was thus modeled rather straightforwardly on the precedent of legal practice.[3]

Transposition of various devices of legal argumentation to debate in rhetoric was already clear with the ancients (e.g., in Aristotle's *Topics* and *Rhetoric,* and in Cicero's *De inventione*).[4] But it was not until 1828 that Richard Whately took a crucial further step in his *Elements of Rhetoric.* Though part of the law of evidence since antiquity, and though tacitly present throughout as a governing factor in disputing practice, the ideas of *burden of proof* and of *presumptions* were first introduced explicitly into the theoretical analysis of *extralegal* argumentation in Whately's treatment of rhetoric. And from that time to the present day they have figured prominently in the theoretical discussions of college debating text books.[5] This continuity of debating with medieval disputation has a solid historical basis. There are good

2. On medieval academic disputations, see A. G. Little and F. Pelster, *Oxford Theology and Theologians* (Oxford, 1934), pp. 29–56. A vivid account of the conduct of scholastic disputations is given in Thomas Gilby, O. P., *Barbara Celarent: A Description of Scholastic Dialectic* (London, 1949); see especially Chapter XXXII, "Formal Debate," pp. 282–293.

3. See, for example, Cicero, *De inventione,* I: 10–16. Cicero's analysis of four types of disputable questions and his description of the successive stages through which a dispute passes is drawn up with a view to the legal situation.

4. A very helpful survey of issues in the theory of argumentation in general is Ch. Perelman and L. Olbrechts-Tyteca, *La Nouvelle Rhetorique: Traité de l'Argumentation,* 2 vols. (Paris, 1958). (Cf. also Perelman's *Rhetorique et philosophie* [Paris, 1952].) Among the older discussions of dialection and its relationship to logic, one which still retains a substantial interest, is Arthur Schopenhauer's "Eristische Dialektik," in *Arthur Schopenhauer: der handschriftliche Nachlass,* ed. by A. Hübscher, vol. III (Frankfurt am Main, 1970), pp. 666–695.

5. See, for example, A. J. Freeley, *Argumentation and Debate,* 2nd ed. (Belmont, Calif., 1966), chap. III, sect. III, "Presumption and Burden of Proof," pp. 30–34. Regarding the literature of rhetoric in general, see the very full bibliography given in Ch. Perelman and L. Olbrechts-Tyteca, *La Nouvelle Rhetorique: Traité de l'Argumentation.*

grounds for holding that the extracurricular disputations of the fifteenth-seventeenth centuries—especially those between rival universities—were the direct precursors of modern intercollegiate debates.[6]

Disputation long survived as a testing method in universities, providing a format for *viva voce* examinations. In German universities it was introduced in the Middle Ages and long continued in standard use to examine doctoral candidates (*Doktoranden*), not only in humanistic fields, but even in the natural sciences.[7] The candidate had to undertake a formal public defense of specified theses against designated opponents, with his professors presiding over the exercise. In later days all this became very much a formality, the candidate having arrived at a friendly understanding with his "opponents" in advance.[8] In the American context such disputation continues in a vestigial form in the final oral examination for graduate degrees, when the candidate defends his thesis or dissertation before a group of his principal professors, who play a dual role: first in the public part of the examination playing out the role of opponents and thereafter deliberating *in camera* as evaluative judges, with the dissertation director acting as counterpart to the determiner of a medieval debate.

It is worthwhile to study the process of disputation closely because it offers—in miniaturized form, as it were—a vivid view of the structure and workings of the validating mechanisms which support our claims to knowledge.

6. See Bromley Smith, "Extracurricular Disputations: 1400–1650," *Quarterly Journal of Speech* 34 (1948): 473–476.

7. See Ewald Horn, "Die Disputationen und Promotionen an den deutschen Universitäten vornehmlich seit dem 16. Jahrhundert," *Centralblatt für Bibliothekswesen* No. 11 (1893); and cf. G. Kaufmann, "Zur Geschichte der academischen Grade und Disputationen," *ibid.*, 11 (1894): 201–225. Compare W. T. Costello, S. J., *The Scholastic Curriculum in Early Seventeenth Century Cambridge* (Cambridge, Mass.; 1958).

8. See the report given by Max Planck of his own experiences at the University of Munich in 1879:

> The *viva voce* examination was followed by the ceremonial *Promotion* in which—according to the regulations of the day—the doctoral candidate had to defend [in disputation] certain theses which he put forward. My "opponents," with whom—as was customary—I had already reached friendly accommodation in advance, were the physicist Carl Runge and the mathematician Adolf Hurwitz. (Max Planck, *Vorträge und Erinnerungen,* 5th ed. [Stuttgart, 1949], p. 4.)

3

2. The structure of a disputation

A disputation, as we have seen, involves three parties: the two disputing adversaries, namely, the *proponent* and his *opponent* (or opposing
respondant), and the *determiner* who presides as referee and judge over
the conduct of the dispute.

The formal structure of the disputation is given in rough outline in
Figure 1.

Figure 1
THE STRUCTURE OF A FORMAL DISPUTATION

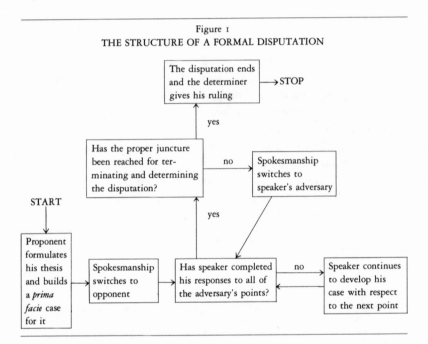

As the disputation proceeds, a sequential series of arguments and
counterarguments is developed around the proponent's initial thesis.
The structure of the overall argument can be set out as a treelike configuration as in Figure 2.

Here T is the basic thesis to be maintained by the proponent. The G_i
are the proponent's supporting considerations adduced as *grounds* in
constructing a *prima facie* case for maintaining the basic thesis T. The
R_{ij} are the counterconsiderations adduced in rebuttal or refutation of

4

Figure 2
THE ALTERNATING PATTERN OF REBUTTAL AND REFUTATION
IN FORMAL DISPUTATION

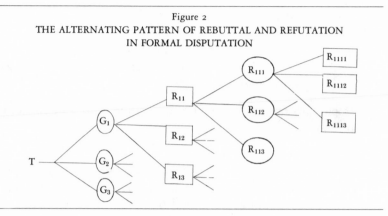

these grounds by the opponent (whose contributions are schematized in boxes, to distinguish them from the proponent's, which are emplaced in ellipses). The R_{ijk} are the proponent's rebuttals of the opponent's R_{ij}. And so on—with a continuing elaboration of reasons *pro* and *con*. Such a rationale-exfoliating tree presents a sequential unfolding of point and counterpoint—a process that probes ever more deeply into the grounding of the proponent's thesis, developing in subtle and comprehensive detail the structure of rational support which he envisages for his focal contention.

3. The formal analysis of dialectical moves and countermoves in disputation

Closer analysis makes it clear that disputation involves a rather stylized routine and is governed by as rigid an etiquette as prevailed in any royal court of the old régime. This fact makes it relatively easy to systematize (at least approximately) the formal moves and countermoves which compose the dialectical fabric of a disputation. The ensuing survey will present—admittedly in a somewhat oversimplified form—the logical structure of the debating moves in a formal disputation. (One point of oversimplification is that the present analysis traces out only one single branch of the exfoliating tree process of Figure 2.)

5

(*i*) *Inventory of fundamental moves* [9]

(1) Categorical assertion

> !*P* for "*P* is the case" or "It is maintained (by me, the assertor) that *P*"

The proponent's opening move of a disputation must take this categorical form.

(2) Cautious assertion

> †*P* for "*P* is the case for all that you (the adversary) have shown" "*P*'s being the case is compatible with everything you've said (i.e., have maintained or conceded)."

Moves of the !-type can be made only by the proponent, those of the †-type only by the opponent.

(3) Provisoed assertion

> *P*/*Q* for "*P* generally (or *usually* or *ordinarily*) obtains provided that *Q*" or "*P* obtains, other things being equal, when *Q* does" or "When *Q*, so *ceteris paribus* does *P*" or "*P* obtains in all (or *most*) ordinary circumstances (or possible worlds) when *Q* does" or "*Q* constitutes *prima facie* evidence for *P*." [10]

NOTE: This move must always be accompanied by one of the two preceding forms of assertion of its operative condition *Q*. Note also that corresponding forms of *denial* arise when ~*P* stands in place of *P*.

In the usual course of things, Americans learn English, fish are not mammals, men are capable of reasoning, birds can fly. And all of these linkages give rise to provisoed assertions. But none of these cir-

---

9. Here "move" means *type* or *kind* of move.

10. Thus *P*/*Q* could be construed as either "*P* obtains in *most* cases of *Q*'s obtaining" or "*P* obtains in all standard (or: *typical*) cases of *Q*'s obtaining." (Note that in either case the transitivity relation *P*/*Q*, *R*/*P* ⊢ *R*/*Q* will *fail* to hold. This alone blocks the prospect of construing the connection at issue as an implication-relationship.) Given that the function of this relationship is dialectic, the second of these constructions seems more appropriate.

cumstances are inevitable. What is at issue in each case is a reasonably safe presumption rather than an airtight guarantee. If A's are B's in the vast majority of cases, if "the general rule" of the situation is such that X's are Y's, or if an F is a G "when things run their normal course," then a corresponding provisoed assertion is generally in order. The relationship at issue is one that deals with what is "normal, natural, and only to be expected." This is not a matter of mere probabilities—of how things go *mostly* or *usually*—rather, it is a matter of how things go *normally* or *as a rule*.

To look upon P/Q as an implication-relation is to slide into an unhelpful misinterpretation. For P/Q *does not* mean that Q implies (entails, assures) that P. Rather, the claim at issue is that it is sensible to suppose that P once Q is given—*sensible* but by no means a *sure* thing. Thus P/Q can be true together with $\sim P/(Q \ \& \ R)$.[11] The addition of a further qualification (proviso) can not only *abrogate* the conditionalized transition to a thesis that obtained under the *status quo ante,* it can render appropriate the transition to its contradictory denial. Accordingly, we cannot reason from such a relationship by invoking a rule of detachment. For clearly if

$$P/Q$$
$$\frac{Q}{P}$$

were an unconditionally valid deductive inference, then we could not possibly have

$$\sim P/(Q \ \& \ R)$$
$$\frac{Q \ \& \ R}{\sim P}$$

be equally valid, without generating a contradiction. This consideration is a decisive impediment to counting the /-relationship as an

11. If the only evidential move available were logical entailment ($\vdash$), rather than this weaker, essentially ampliative stroke-relationship, then the very reason for being of disputation would be undermined. For in a strictly deductive argument, the conclusion cannot be epistemically weaker than its weakest premiss. This would preclude any prospect of building up a case for an epistemically frail conclusion from relatively firm premisses (just as in inductive reasoning), and exactly this is one of the key aims of disputation. This fact constrains the grounding-relationship at issue to be of less than deductive strength.

implication-relation. It represents a linkage that is *presumptive* rather than deductively airtight. This failure of the detachment principle means that in *dialectical* (as opposed to *deductive*) reasoning an assessment of the cognitive standing of a thesis can never leave its probative origins behind altogether.

For simplicity we shall suppose throughout the present chapter that moves of the form X/Y are always "correct" in the setting of a disputation; that the disputants cannot make—or perhaps, rather, are debarred by the determiner from making—erroneous claims regarding purely evidential relationships. We thus exclude the prospect of incorrect contentions about the merely probative issue of what constitutes evidence for what. Accordingly, the disputing parties can avoid addressing themselves to the proprieties of the reasoning and need only attend to issues of substance in the development of the argumentation. (This assumption eliminates various complications that do not really matter for present purposes.)

In consequence of this supposition, certain theoretically feasible exchanges cannot arise, as for example:

proponent	opponent
1. $!P$	$\sim P/Q$ & $\dagger Q$
2. P/Q & $!Q$	

For this exchange clearly involves a disagreement (as between P/Q and $\sim P/Q$) of the kind that runs afoul of our assumptive proscription of error regarding evidential claims of the form X/Y.

The orthodox opening of a disputation is for the proponent to formulate and assert his thesis (in the categorial mode $!T$). The opponent may then offer an opposing challenge ($\dagger \sim T$ as launched against $!T$), and the proponent thereupon proceeds to develop his supporting argument for it, offering one (or possibly more) grounding contentions such as: T/Q & $!Q$.[12]

With this survey of the *basic* moves needed to get a disputation

---

12. In the actual practice a scholastic disputation was sometimes complicated by the practice of (in effect) a role-reversal which assigned to the opponent the task of carrying the burden of proof in establishing the falsity of the proponent's thesis. See Thomas Gilby, *Barbara Celarent: A Description of Scholastic Debate*, pp. 282–293. The proponent would open with a state-

started safely in hand, let us now turn to a consideration of the dialectical moves and countermoves that constitute the development of the argumentation at issue.

(ii) Dialectical countermoves: countermoves to fundamental moves

(a) Countermoves to categorical assertion or counterassertion

The following two responses may be offered by the opponent in reply against !P.

1. Challenge or cautious denial

$$\dagger \sim P$$

NOTE: this is simply the qualified assertion of the contradictory of an asserted thesis. Such a challenge traditionally took the form "Please prove P" (faveas probare P).

2. Provisoed denial

$$\sim P/Q \ \& \ \dagger Q, \text{ for some suitable } Q$$

Whenever the proponent has made moves of the form $!X_1$, $!X_2$, . . . , $!X_n$, and some thesis Y is a logical consequence of these X_i (X_1, X_2, . . . , $X_n \vdash Y$), then the opponent can offer a challenge of the form $\dagger \sim Y$ or a provisoed denial of the form $\sim Y/Z \ \& \ \dagger Z$. Thus if $P \vdash Q$, the proponent's categorical assertion $!P$ can be met by the opponent either by a direct challenge $\dagger \sim Q$ or by the provisoed denial $\sim P/Q \ \& \ \dagger Q$. Challenges can thus be issued not only against categorical assertions themselves, but also against their logical consequences. Such consequence-challenge is simply an extended form of a challenge issued against a thesis itself.

In line with these two possibilities, a formal disputation always opens on one of the following two patterns:

ment of the disputed thesis (and perhaps some grounds for it). The opponent would then take on the probative burden of maintaining a contrary (sed contra est!) of the proponent's thesis. But this was simply a matter of a functional role-interchange within the same framework.

9

Pattern I		Pattern II	
proponent	opponent	proponent	opponent
(1) !P	$\dagger\sim P$	!P	$\sim P/Q$ & $\dagger Q$
(2) P/Q & !Q			

On both patterns the proponent opens with a categorical assertion (a statement of his thesis), on the lines of the traditional formula "I maintain (*affirmo*) that P." With Pattern I the opponent denies this thesis—or, more strictly, denies that the proponent has any adequate entitlement for his claim: "I deny (*nego*) that P [can be maintained]." The proponent must then proceed (as at Step (2)) with the setting out of his case. With Pattern II, on the other hand, the opponent proceeds straightaway to launch a counterattack on the proponent's thesis (in the form of a provisoed counterassertion).

A categorical denial of the form !$\sim P$ is simply the categorical assertion of $\sim P$. It may thus be met by the opponent by one of the countermoves to categorical assertion, viz., either by the cautious denial $\dagger P$ (equivalent to $\dagger\sim\sim P$), or by the provisoed denial P/Q & $\dagger Q$.

It is worth noting that the opponent's moves can always be put in the form of a question: the challenge "$\dagger\sim P$" as "What entitles you to claim P?" or the provisoed denial "$\sim P/Q$ & $\dagger Q$" as "How can you maintain P seeing that $\sim P/Q$ and for all you've shown Q?" This interrogative approach is in fact always possible with opponent's moves. Accordingly, the opponent was also often characterized as the questioner (*interrogans*).

(b) Countermoves to cautious assertion or denial

The following responses may be offered to $\dagger P$

1. Categorical counterassertion

$$!\sim P$$

2. Provisoed counterassertion

$$\sim P/Q \ \& \ !Q, \text{ for some suitable } Q$$

NOTE: (1) Because they involve components of the form !X, these moves are available only to the proponent.

NOTE: (2) It is necessary to preclude the repetitive—indeed circular sequence:

proponent	opponent
$!P$	$\dagger\sim P$
$!P$	

This blockage is accomplished by adopting a special rule to proscribe the simple *repetition* of a previous move. The reason for such a non-repetition rule lies deep in the rationale of the process of disputation. A disputation must be *progressive:* it must continually advance into new terrain. Since its aim is to deepen the grounding of the contentions at issue, it must always endeavor to *improve* upon the reasoning already laid out, in the interests of achieving greater sophistication. Mere repetition would frustrate the aim of the enterprise.

A cautious denial (or *challenge*) of the form $\dagger\sim P$ is simply the cautious assertion of the negative thesis $\sim P$. It may thus be met either by

1. The categorical counterassertion

$$!\sim\sim P \text{ or equivalently } !P$$

or

2. A provisoed counterassertion of the form

$$P/Q \ \& \ !Q$$

Cautious denial being available only to the opponent, these countermoves are available only to the proponent. The following sequence represents a typical exchange:

proponent	opponent
$P/Q \ \& \ !Q$	$\sim P/(Q \ \& \sim R) \ \& \ \dagger(Q \ \& \sim R)$
$!\sim(Q \ \& \sim R) = !(\sim Q \ v \ R)$	$[Q, \sim Q \ v \ R \vdash R] \ \& \ \dagger\sim R$
$!R$	

(c) Countermoves to provisoed assertion or denial

A provisoed assertion P/Q can only be maintained in the context of a nonprovisoed assertion of Q, be it the categorial $!Q$ (by the proponent) or the cautious $\dagger Q$ (by the opponent). Beyond attacking these through the aforementioned responses, the following further responses may be offered in reply against P/Q as such:

1. Weak distinction (or weak exception)

$\sim P/(Q \ \& \ R) \ \& \ \dagger(Q \ \& \ R)$, for some suitable R

NOTE (1): Again, this move is available only to the opponent.
NOTE (2): In the special case of $R = Q$ this move comes to $\sim P/Q \ \&$
$\dagger Q$. But this cannot be, given our convention that grounding moves
of the form X/Y are always "correct," $\sim P/Q$ cannot arise in the face of
P/Q. Hence R must represent some genuine qualification to Q, so that
the move from Q to $Q \ \& \ R$ constitutes an advance in the discussion.

2. Strong distinction (or strong exception)

$\sim P/(Q \ \& \ R) \ \& \ !(Q \ \& \ R)$

NOTE (1): Again, this move is available only to the proponent.
NOTE (2): The same situation as with Note (2) of case (1) recurs.

Distinction must be understood in the light of the earlier observation that P/Q may well be perfectly compatible with $\sim P/(Q \ \& \ R)$. In
putting forward the latter in the face of the former, a disputant may
well be prepared to concede that Q in itself militates for P, but insist
that the operative proviso at issue is not Q itself but $Q \ \& \ R$, and that
this latter militates against rather than for P. Distinction is the most
characteristic and the most *creative* of dialectical moves.[13] The exploration of requisite provisos through the discovery of necessary distinctions is thus a highly important aspect of inquiry.

Consider just an example. The history of modern science has again
and again led to situations of the following structure: An old theory
emerges as inadequate, in that it can be shown to hold only as a
special case under particular circumstances, as Newtonian principles
hold only under those special conditions in which relativistic or quan-
tum effects can be ignored. In such cases the discovery of the needed
restrictive provisoes—and the indication of the distinctions that must
be drawn to obtain a scientifically viable account—has an emphatically dialectical aspect.

Provisoed denial is simply the provisoed assertion of a contra-

13. Recognition of the central role of distinctions in the dialectical enterprise—based on the
division (*dihairesis*) of key concepts—goes back at least to the Socrates of Plato's *Phaedrus* and is
doubtless present in the theory and practice of the early Sophists.

dicting thesis. It can thus be countered by moves of the same type as the preceding.

Consider a dialectical exchange of the form:

proponent	opponent
(n) . . . & !P	†~P
(n + 1) P/Q & !Q	~P/(Q & R) & †(Q & R)

A situation of this sort exhibits the traditional distinction between (i) an opponent's rejection at step (n + 1) of the *consequence relationship* (*consequentia*) by insisting on drawing a due distinction (as per the traditional formula *nego consequens et distinguo:* "I deny the consequent and distinguish"), and (ii) the move made at step (n) in simply denying the *consequent* P itself. Accordingly, the whole complex of the opponent's two-move posture here would be captured by the traditional formula *nego consequens et consequetiam* ("I deny both the *consequent* and the *consequence*").

This completes the survey of the countermoves to the three *basic* dialectical moves. Before turning to the countermoves against complex ones, a brief historical digression is in order.

It is an important, but in the final analysis accidental, feature of scholastic disputation that it was carried on in *syllogistic* form. Our present discussion could readily be recast to accommodate this circumstance. It must be understood, however, that the categorial propositions recurring in the premises may be subject to the special qualification "usually"—i.e., standardly or ordinarily—which gives them a tentative and provisional "until it's shown otherwise" status. In the disputational setting this special qualification must be understood as present throughout, be it tacitly or explicitly.

When disputation is cast in a syllogistic format, various dialectical moves take on a characteristically concordant aspect. For example, if a proponent's thesis takes the form

$$!P = !\text{ All } \alpha \text{ is } \beta$$

then a provisoed denial of the type ~P/Q & †Q could take the form of the argument:

$$\frac{\dagger Q = \dagger[(\text{Some } \alpha \text{ is } \gamma) \ \& \ @(\text{No } \gamma \text{ is } \beta)]}{\therefore \sim P = \text{Some } \alpha \text{ is not } \beta}$$

where $@$ is the all-things-being-equal operator. (In the absence of $@$ the relationship at issue would be *deductive* rather than merely *presumptive,* as wanted. As it stands the $@$-qualifier always carries over from a universal premiss to the conclusion itself.) [14] The opponent's problem here is, of course, the finding of some suitable middle term γ that would render the premiss true, or at least plausible.

Again, distinction would also have to proceed syllogistically. It does so by *dividing* the middle term, splitting it in two by drawing a suitable distinction. Thus let us suppose that P/Q takes the syllogistic form

$$\frac{Q = [(\text{All } \alpha \text{ is } \gamma) \ \& \ @(\text{All } \gamma \text{ is } \beta)]}{\therefore P = \text{All } \alpha \text{ is } \beta}$$

Then in reply an apposite distinction might be drawn with respect to γ in such a way that the following syllogistic inference is warranted:

$$\frac{Q' = [(\text{Some } \alpha \text{ is } \gamma\text{-that-is-}\delta) \ \& \ @(\text{No } \gamma\text{-that-is-}\delta \text{ is } \beta)]}{\therefore P = \text{Some } \alpha \text{ is not } \beta}$$

Note that in offering this reply the adversary need not deny the opposing claim that *"Usually:* All γ is β"; he simply shifts the focus of attention from the γ in general to those γ that are specifically δ, maintaining that (usually) none of *these* are β.

For purposes of our discussion we shall, however, treat it as an accidental and negligible complication that classical scholastic disputation was carried on in terms of specifically syllogistic argumentation. Our analysis of the basic dialectical issues may without damage consider this to be an inessential point of detail.

14. The introduction of this $@$ qualifier leads back to the scholastic conception of a qualified or restricted universal, the universal *ut nunc* regarding which, see John Oesterle, "The Significance of the Universal *ut nunc"* in J. A. Weisheipl (ed.), *The Dignity of Science* (Washington, D.C., 1961), pp. 27–38.

(iii) Dialectical countermoves: countermoves to complex moves

(d) Countermoves to a provisoed denial

A *provisoed denial* of the form $\sim P/Q$ & $\dagger Q$ may be met by the proponent by attacking either of its two components. It can be countered either by attacking the cautious denial $\dagger Q$ along the two lines of (b) above (viz., a categorical counterassertion $!\sim Q$ or a conditionalized counterassertion $\sim Q/(R$ & $!R)$, or else by attacking the provisoed assertion $\sim P/Q$. This latter attack can take the additional form of a strong distinction: $P/(Q$ & $S)$ & $!(Q$ & $S)$.

(e) Countermoves to provisoed counterassertion

A provisoed counterassertion of the form $\sim P/Q$ & $!Q$ may be met by the opponent's attacking either component. It may thus be countered either by attacking the categorical assertion $!Q$ (either by the cautious denial $\dagger\sim Q$ or by the provisoed denial $\sim Q/(R$ & $\dagger R)$, or else by attacking the provisoed assertion $\sim P/Q$. This latter attack can take the additional form of a weak distinction: $P/(Q$ & $S)$ & $\dagger(Q$ & $S)$.

(f) Countermoves to a weak distinction

A weak distinction of the form $\sim P/(Q$ & $R)$ & $\dagger(Q$ & $R)$ may be met by the proponent's attacking either component. It may thus be countered by attacking $\dagger(Q$ & $R)$—either with a categorical counterassertion $!\sim(Q$ & $R)$ or by a provisoed counterassertion of the form $\sim(Q$ & $R)/S$ & $!S$—or else by countering $\sim P/(Q$ & $R)$ by drawing a strong distinction: $P/(Q$ & R & $S)$ & $!(Q$ & R & $S)$.

(g) Countermoves to a strong distinction

A strong distinction of the form $\sim P/(Q$ & $R)$ & $!(Q$ & $R)$ may be met by the opponent's attacking either component. It may thus be countered by attacking $!(Q$ & $R)$—either with the challenge $\dagger\sim(Q$ & $R)$ or by a provisoed denial of the form $\sim(Q$ & $R)/S$ & $\dagger S$—or else by countering $\sim P/(Q$ & $R)$ by drawing a weak distinction of the form $P/(Q$ & R & $T)$ & $\dagger(Q$ & R & $T)$.

By compiling these various possibilities one arrives at a more fine-grained view of the structure of a formal disputation, filling in with greater detail the schematic picture given in Figures 1 and 2. However, the discussion of the present section appears in this context as something of an oversimplification. It envisages making countermoves one at a time. But the actual practice of disputation is somewhat more free and easy, and permits several concurrent challenges or responses.

As a concrete illustration of the kind of disputational process at issue here, consider the following example from a "formal debate" drawing on themes to be discussed at greater length in Chapter Six.

prop.: We can know things by sensation, as, for example, [I know that *this* is a human hand]. Here [] = P. Thus !P.

opp.: You don't know that's a hand if you are not certain of it, and for all you've said [you aren't certain that that's a hand]. Here [] = Q. Thus ~P/Q & †Q.

prop.: But I *am* certain that this is a hand. Thus !~Q.

opp.: But you can't be certain if [your senses mislead you in this case], and for all you've said, your senses may be misleading you. Here [] = R. Thus Q/R & †R.

prop.: But my senses are clearly not misleading me in this case. Thus !~R.

opp.: But [your senses have misled you in other cases somewhat like this one], and so they might be misleading you in this case as well. Here [] = S. Thus R/S & †S.

prop.: My senses have misled me in cases similar to this one, but [these cases were different in certain key respects]. And I insist that this case is different in such respects, so that these cases have not been *just* like this one, in which, I maintain, my senses aren't misleading me. Here [] = T. Thus ~R/(S & T) & !(S & T).

opp.: But [it is surely *possible* that your senses might err in this case], and so you cannot claim knowledge here. Here [] = U. Thus Q/U & †U.

prop.: [The possibility you speak of—that a human hand is not actually at issue—is only a *conjectural* one]; I deny that it is *real*. And purely conjectural, imaginary possibilities don't block knowledge. Here [] = V. Thus ~Q/(U & V) & !(U & V).

The cut and thrust of this sample controversy may help to illustrate how the present formalism can be used to capture a series of exchanges of the type at issue in a formal disputation. The structure of the argumentation runs as follows:

proponent	opponent
(1) $!P$	$\sim P/Q$ & $\dagger Q$
(2) $!\sim Q$	Q/R & $\dagger R$
(3) $!\sim R$	R/S & $\dagger S$
(4) $\sim R/(S$ & $T)$ & $!(S$ & $T)$	Q/U & $\dagger U$
(5) $\sim Q/(U$ & $V)$ & $!(U$ & $V)$	

Note that at step (4) the opponent does not reply to the proponent's latest move, but rather resumes his attack on the proponent's step (2) contention, from a different point of departure. This step effectively concedes the adequacy of the proponent's response at this point. And note also the structural isomorphism of the proponent's moves at step (4) and (5), both of which respond to the opponent's moves not by way of a direct denial, but by way of a distinction.

4. Probative asymmetries

It is worth stressing that there are certain crucial role-governed asymmetries or disparities in position between the parties in a disputation:

1. The proponent must inaugurate the disputation. And he must do so with a categorial assertion of the thesis he proposes to defend.
2. All countermoves involving categorical assertion (conditionalized counterassertion, strong distinction) are open to the proponent alone. Moreover, *the proponent's every move involves some categorical assertion:* he is the party on whom it is incumbent to take a committal stance at every juncture. The "burden of proof" lies on his side throughout.
3. All countermoves involving a challenge or cautious denial (including provisoed detail and weak distinction) are open to the opponent alone. Moreover, *the opponent's every move involves some challenge or cautious denial:* he is the party who need merely call claims into

17

question and carries no responsibility for making any positive claims.[15]

The process of disputation thus exhibits a significant dialectical asymmetry. A disparity or imbalance of probative position is built into the proponent's role as supporter and the opponent's as sceptical denier.

Every step taken by the proponent involves a commitment of some sort, and the proponent is liable for the defense of all of these—he is vulnerable at every point to a call to make good his claims. The opponent, on the other hand, need make no positive claims at all. He need merely challenge the proponent's claims, and his work is adequately done if he succeeds in bringing to light the inadequacy of some one of the claims on which the proponent's case rests.

In this regard, *formal disputation* with its opposing $!T$ by $\dagger T$ differs from a *symmetrically contradictory debate* that opposes $!\sim T$ to $!T$. The latter situation is typical of modern collegiate debating, where each side undertakes to defend one member of a pair of mutually contradictory theses. This situation gives rise to what is, in effect, simply a *pair* of concurrent and interlocked disputations: One contender is proponent for T to his adversary's opponentship, and this adversary is proponent of $\sim T$ to his adversary's opponentship. On each side we have an attempt to build up a cogent and persuasive case in the face of sceptical objections from the other. The situation that results here poses no theoretical innovations. It simply reflects the evolution of disputation into a variant form of controversy that makes for a situation of probative symmetry between the parties.

5. The microstructure of the dialectic of disputation

A disputation involves a stylized sequence of moves and countermoves that locks the participants into a rigorously programmed minuet of well-determined steps. The various combinatorial possibilities that

15. Such a challenge can always be put into the form of a question: "But just what entitles you to maintain . . . ?" Disputation can thus be carried on in a question-and-answer process. Aristotle sometimes approaches the matter in this way in Book VII of the *Topics*.

can arise will conform in structure to a circumscribed sequence of admissible exchanges, as set out in the flow-diagram of Figure 3.

Since this process is intrinsically nonterminating (as the flow-diagram contains wholly closed circuits), there must be some additional rules—extrinsic to the dialectical process itself—for fixing a stopping point to the process. Various alternatives are possible here: e.g., a predesignated total number of exchanges, a fixed period of time, surrender by one of the parties for reasons of frustration or exhaustion, etc. (The rule should, however, be such that the proponent gets the last word.)

The flow-diagram at issue is *indeterministic*. At every stage there are choice-points that present genuine alternatives. It remains to be fixed whether the disputation is to be strictly *linear* (in that only one of these moves can be made at every step) or ramified—i.e., whether several *concurrent* attacking or defending moves might be offered. Only in this second—and more orthodox—case would we get a branching diagram as in Figure 2 above.

Figure 3
THE SEQUENCING OF MOVES AND COUNTERMOVES
PROPONENT   *OPPONENT*

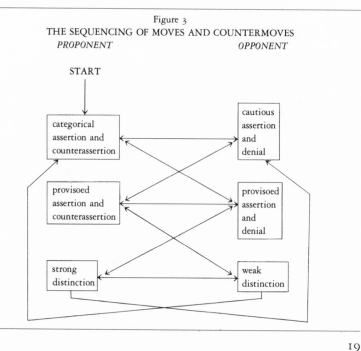

It must also be stressed that the diagram needs to be supplemented by the (already mentioned) blockage rule which precludes the proponent from reasserting (or the opponent for rechallenging) something he has effectively asserted (or challenged) before.[16] Examples of such blocked sequences are:

proponent	opponent
!P	†~P
!~~P = !P	

Or again:

proponent	opponent
!P	†~P
P/Q & !Q	†~Q
Q/P & !P	

6. The determination (adjudication) of a disputation

The preceding analysis has stressed the fundamental disparity in probative position of the two rival parties in a disputation. The ultimate burden of proof rests squarely with the proponent. He alone is entitled—and indeed required—at every stage of the proceedings to make moves that involve a definite commitment (and so have a component of the form !X).

Accordingly, the proponent alone maintains an ever-changing variety of *commitments* during the course of the disputation—a shifting constellation of theses to whose defense he stands committed. The issue of such commitment needs closer scrutiny.

A proponent *discharges* a commitment when he "exchanges" it for another through a sequence of the form:

proponent	opponent
. . . & !P	†~P
P/Q & !Q	

16. Every asertion (!X) is effective, but a challenge (†X) is effective only when it provokes a response from the proponent.

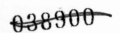

Here the proponent has, as it were, exchanged his initial commitment to defend P for one to defend its supportive pillar Q instead. When the challenge to a *direct* commitment to X (of the form $!X$) is taken up and transformed into an *indirect* commitment to X via some Y—then the initial commitment to X is "discharged." (Of course, all the logical consequences of discharged commitments must also be taken to be discharged.)

An opponent *concedes* a committed thesis—tacitly, to be sure—when he subjects it to a distinction. Thus consider the sequence:

proponent	opponent
P/Q & $!Q$	$\sim P/(Q$ & $R)$ & $\dagger(Q$ & $R)$

The opponent here concedes Q in switching the ground from considering the acceptability of P in the face of Q to considering its status in the face of Q & $R,$ the combination of Q conjoined with some other thesis R. Again, the opponent concedes a committed thesis when he fails to attack it when given as an opportunity to do so. Thus consider the sequence

proponent	opponent
$!P$	$\sim P/Q$ & $\dagger Q$
$P/(Q$ & $R)$ & $!(Q$ & $R)$	$\dagger \sim R$

By ignoring Q—which he had, moreover, insinuated in his initial attack—the opponent concedes it.

Given the ever-shifting pattern of commitment on the proponent's part (undertaking new commitments, discharging old ones, having others conceded), there will at each stage be a (constantly changing) group of *living commitments* on his part. This is illustrated in the following example:

proponent	opponent
(1) $!P$	$\sim P/Q$ & $\dagger Q$
(2) $P/\sim Q$ & $!\sim Q$	$\sim P/(\sim Q$ & $R)$ & $\dagger(\sim Q$ & $R)$
(3) $!\sim(\sim Q$ & $R)$	$\dagger R$
(4) $\sim R/S$ & $!S$	

The changing pattern of commitments at issue here is shown in the accompanying table.

THE CHANGING PATTERN OF COMMITMENT

	proponent's undischarged commitments at this stage *	opponent's (cumulative) concessions at this stage	proponent's living commitments at this stage (undischarged commitments that are *not* conceded)
(1)	P	—	P
(2)	$\sim Q$	$\sim Q$	—
(3)	$\sim Q, \sim R$ **	$\sim Q$	$\sim R$
(4)	$\sim Q, S$	$\sim Q$	S

*The proponent's undischarged commitments are exactly those theses which (together with their logical consequences) the opponent is free to challenge under the rule of countermove (a) above (see p. 9).

** In the presence of a commitment to $\sim Q$, the commitment to $\sim(\sim Q \ \& \ R)$, or equivalently $Q \ v \sim R$, is tantamount to a commitment to $\sim R$.

Note that at step (3) we need to invoke the special rule: *The opponent may always challenge the logical consequences of any undischarged commitments.* Instead of challenging a thesis as such, the opponent can
challenge one of its consequences (be it a categorical consequence or
a conditional consequence in the face of other commitments). Moreover, it is certainly open to an opponent to *revoke* a concession at any
stage. Thus at step (4) the opponent's move could return to one part
of his very first intervention at step (1) to reiterate the challenge †Q
(which was ineffective at that initial stage, since the proponent re-
plied to $\sim P/Q$ and ignored †Q). In choosing to attack $P/\sim Q$ at step
(2), the opponent *suspended,* but did not *resign* his right to attack the
proponent's contention $!\sim Q$. In the interim, however, the old dictum
that "silence implies consent" prevails *pro tem.* The revocation of a
concession on the part of an opponent restores it to the status of a
commitment on the part of the proponent.

Moreover, an opponent can always return to a previous "bone of
contention" of an earlier stage of the controversy, from a fresh point
of departure, as per the sequence:

proponent	opponent
!P	$\sim P/Q$ & $\dagger Q$
!$\sim Q$	$\sim P/R$ & $\dagger R$

In taking this tactic of ignoring a response by returning to a previous juncture, the opponent pays the price of making a concession, at any rate *pro tem* (as with $\sim Q$ in the present case).

The "determination" of a disputation is, of course, a pivotally important issue, governing the entire process that issues in this climactic culmination. When the dispute ends, the determiner uses the following standards in adjudging the dispute with a view to assessing what adversary deserves to be counted as the victor:

1. A *formal* criterion with reference to *the avoidance of illicit moves:* Did the proponent argue in a circle? Did the opponent challenge theses which he had already called into question before? Did anyone perpetrate formal errors in reasoning?

If all's well as to point 1 (as one would ordinarily expect to be the case), then a different criterion comes into play.

2. A *material* criterion with reference to assessing the extent to which the opponent drove the proponent into implausible commitments. This is a matter of assessing the plausibility (absolute plausibility or perhaps simply the plausibility relative to the initial thesis) of the proponents's undischarged and unconceded commitments.

This evaluation process serves to determine the strategy of disputation. *The proponent has to cover his commitments in a maximally plausible way;* the opponent tries to force him into more difficult commitments by introducing cleverly contrived distinctions that push his adversary in this direction.[17] (In terminating a dispute a clear distinction must, of course, be made between those of the opponent's concessions which represent theses he has had an opportunity to attack, those that he has declined and those which he has not yet—at this stage—had adequate opportunity to attack.) In a well-conducted disputation, one will

17. This idea that a successful course of dialectical reasoning should not argue to a conclusion from less plausible premises was already stressed by Aristotle in the *Topics* (e.g., at 161b19–34).

23

always be able to extract by analysis of the exchanges of the pro-con tabulation a good (though certainly not necessarily a *deductively* valid) *argument*—a unilateral line of reasoning in support of a thesis.[18] And "victory" is determined by how cogent a case the proponent manages to make relative to the possibilities at his disposal through the mechanisms of plausibility and presumption.

The pivotal facet of the "determination" of a disputation is thus its crucial dependence upon a means for evaluating the plausibility (acceptability) of the theses upon which the proponent is—in the end—driven by the opponent to rest his case. This is what fixes the aim and object of the whole enterprise—and indeed determines its entire strategy. For the proponent is ever striving to lead his case towards the secure ground of plausible contentions and the opponent is ever seeking to prevent his reaching any such safe harbor.

The preceding deliberations present a somewhat overstylized picture of the disputational venture, reflecting the historical realities of a more variegated and loose-jointed process which has here been regimented into a tighter and more stylized form. Such a sharpening—or oversimplification, if you insist—does, however, help to bring into clearer relief the general structure of the process of disputation and to illuminate the central issue it poses for an understanding of the dialectics of rational controversy. This disputational version provides the paradigm model of dialectics for the purposes of our present deliberations.

18. This is why a disputational model of formal proof can readily be developed. See Appendix 2 of Chapter Four.

2 Some dialectical tools: burden of proof, presumption, and plausibility

1. The legal origins of the idea of burden of proof

No conception is more critical to a proper understanding of dialectical issues than that of the burden of proof.

The idea of "burden of proof" (*onus probandi*) is at root a legal conception. It functions in the context of an adversary proceeding where one party is endeavoring to establish and another to rebut some charge (involving guilt, responsibility, default, etc.) before a neutral adjudicative tribunal. The very phrase (*onus probandi*) derives from classical Roman law. It has to do with the ground rules of probative procedure, specifically the division of the labor of argumentation between plaintiff and defendant, which specify tasks regarding the marshalling of evidence. Under the Roman system, nothing was conceded in legal actions as admitted: the plaintiff, as the initiating agent in laying a charge, had his case to make out first (*agenti incumbit probatio*), then the defendant's countercase was argued on his *exceptio,* then again the plaintiff's on his *replicatio,* and so on. The burden rested with the plaintiff in civil and with the state (as surrogate plaintiff) in criminal cases. Throughout, the "burden of proof" lay with the side active in making the allegations, subject to the fundamental rule: *necessitas probandi incumbit ei qui dicit non ei qui negat* ("The need for proof lies with him who affirms not him who denies").[1]

Various aspects of Anglo-American legal procedure derive from this conception. The principle that the accused is "innocent until proven guilty" is, in effect, a straightforward device for allocating the burden of proof. And the "Scots verdict" of *not proven* affords a way of saying that the burden has been discharged in part, sufficiently for the correlative presumption (of innocence) to come to an end, without, however, an actual proof of guilt having been formally established.[2]

The idea of burden of proof is interlocked with that of evidence. The concept articulates a basic rule of the evidential game. To say that the burden of proof rests with a certain side is to say that it is up to that side to bring in the evidence to make its case. Thus in the face of the presumption of innocence, the prosecution is, in criminal law, obliged to present to the court at least a *prima facie* case for maintaining the guilt of the accused. This is to be accomplished by furnishing information sufficient to show the guilt of the accused in the absence of counterevidence. In California, for example, a level of blood alcohol in excess of 1/10 percent (as indicated by a blood or breath test administered to a driver at the scene of an arrest) is considered *prima facie* evidence of driving while intoxicated. But, of course, the development of such a *prima facie* case is capable of rebuttal by the deployment of further evidence (e.g., its being shown that the inebriated person was merely a passenger of the vehicle, not its driver).[3]

This outline points towards a fact which careful students of the matter have long realized. Burden of proof involves two rather different sorts of things. One authority has put the matter as follows:

> In modern law the phrase "burden of proof" may mean one of two things, which are often confused—the burden of establishing the proposition at issue on which the case depends, and the burden of producing

1. Sir Courtenay Peregrine Ilbert, art. "Evidence," *Encyclopaedia Britannica* (11th ed.), vol. 10, pp. 11–21 (see p. 15).

2. These issues and many others that bear upon the concerns of this chapter are treated in that classic work on legal reasoning: J. H. Wigmore, *The Principles of Judicial Proof* (Boston, 1913; with numerous later editions).

3. For a good exposition of the legal issues, see Richard A. Epstein, "Pleadings and Presumptions," *The University of Chicago Law Review*, 40 (1973/4): 556–582.

evidence on any particular point either at the beginning or at a later stage of the case. The burden in the former sense ordinarily rests on the plaintiff or prosecutor. The burden in the latter sense, that of going forward with evidence on a particular point, may shift from side to side as the case proceeds. The general rule is that he who alleges a fact must prove it, whether the allegation is construed in affirmative or negative terms.[4]

Accordingly there are really two distinct, albeit related, conceptions of "burden of proof":

(1) The *probative burden of an initiating assertion* (initiating I-burden of proof). The basic rule is: "Whichever side initiates the assertion of a thesis within the dialectical situation has the burden of supporting it in argument." The champion of a thesis—like the champion of a medieval joust—must be prepared to maintain his side in the face of the opposing challenges. This burden of *agenti incumbit probatio* remains constant throughout.

(2) The *evidential burden of further reply in the face of contrary considerations* (evidential E-burden of proof). Whenever considerations of suitably weighty evidential bearing have been adduced, this argument may be taken as standing provisionally until some sufficient reply has been made against it in turn. Thus the opponent of any contention—be it an assertion or a denial—always has the "burden of further reply." This "burden of going forward with evidence (or counterevidence)," as it is sometimes called, may shift from side to side as the dialectic of controversy proceeds.

The former mode (initiating I-burden) is static and rests with the inugurating side constantly and throughout; the latter (evidential E-burden) involves the idea that a suitably weighty amount of evidence can manage to *shift* the burden from one side to the other as the course of argumentation proceeds. This second type of burden is crucial. It embodies the imperative of "advancing the argument" in a meaningful way, carrying the discussion forward beyond a particular stage of its development. And in doing so, it implements one of the key functions of the process of controversy.

4. Sir Courtenay Ilbert, "Evidence," p. 15.

Thus consider the following exchange in formal disputation:

proponent	opponent
. . . & $!P$	$\sim P/Q$ & $\dagger Q$

Here the opponent has adduced a suitable item of counterevidence (viz., Q) against the proponent's contention P and so the evidential ball is "thrown back into the proponent's court," so to speak. Q is (*ex hypothesi*) a countervailing factor that turns the table of presumption against P. But if the proponent now proceeds to the response $\sim Q/R$ & $!R$, for some suitable piece of evidence R, then he has once again shifted the E-burden to the opponent's side.

In the dialectic of controversy the burden of proof in this evidential sense of further reply (E-burden of proof) shifts back and forth between the parties in accordance with the evidential position of their case at each stage. The key idea here is that of adducing probative considerations whose force is "sufficient" to reverse the burden of proof, shifting the weight of argument from one side to the other.

2. Presumption and the concept of a provisionally adequate case

The conception of a *prima facie* case is intimately connected with that of burden of proof in the evidential, E-burden-of-proof version of this idea. A *prima facie* case is, in effect, one that succeeds in *shifting* the burden of proof—it "demands an answer" from the adversary and, until one is forthcoming, inclines the balance of favorable judgment to its side. To make out a *prima facie* case for one's contention is to adduce considerations whose evidential weight is such that—in the absence of countervailing considerations—the "reasonable presumption" is now in its favor, and the burden of proof (in the E-sense of an adequate reply that "goes forward with [counter] evidence") is now incumbent on the opposing party.

In accordance with this line of thought, we may introduce the idea of an "evidentially sufficient" contention (ES-contention), namely a contention that succeeds in effecting a shift in the burden of proof

28

with respect to the thesis on whose behalf it is brought forward. Unlike *decisively* established contentions (self-evident protocols or the like), such ES-contentions will in general be defeasible. They do not stand unshakeable, established once and for all, but only provisionally and "until further notice"—or rather until considerations have been adduced that succeed in setting them aside. Such ES-contentions must be of a sort that (1) there is a substantial presumption of truth in their favor, and (2) the evidential force they are able to lend to the thesis in whose behalf they are adduced is sufficiently weighty that the burden of proof is shifted in its favor.

This idea of evidential sufficiency is closely connected with that of the *weight* of the burden of proof or of the *strength* of presumption (to look at the other side of the coin). British law, for example, adopts different standards of proof in criminal and civil cases. In criminal cases guilt must be established "beyond reasonable doubt"; in civil cases it is sufficient to show that the defendant is guilty "on the balance of probabilities." And both standards are flexible: in criminal cases, "What is reasonable doubt . . . [should vary] in practice according to . . . the punishment which may be awarded."[5] Moreover "the standard [of proof for cases of fraud] is the civil one of preponderance of probabilities, but what is 'probable' depends upon the heinousness of what is alleged . . . 'in proportion as the offense is grave, so ought the proof to be clear' . . . ."[6] In general (and in disputation as well) what is evidentially sufficient in shifting a burden of proof will hinge on the inherent seriousness of the contention at issue.

It cannot be emphasized too strongly that the idea of burden of proof is not a strictly *logical* concept. Logic in itself has no dealings with the issue of probative obligations or even with the (categorical) truth status or presumptive truth status of propositions—its concern with truth is wholly in hypothetical mode ("If certain theses are [assumed to be] true, then certain others must also be [assumed to be] true"). Rather than being a *logical* concept, burden of proof is a *methodological* one. It has to do not with valid or invalid reasoning, but with probative argumentation in dialectical situations. The workings

5. R. A. Epstein, "Pleadings and Presumptions," see pp. 558–559.
6. *Philipson on Evidence*, 11th edition (London, 1970), p. 230.

29

of the conception of burden of proof represent a *procedural or regulative principle of rationality* in the conduct of argumentation, a ground rule, as it were, of the process of rational controversy—a fundamental condition of the whole enterprise.

3. Presumption and burden of proof

While the fundamental burden of proof always inclines against the interlocutor who presents a thesis for acceptance, one must, of course, make it *possible* for him to build a substantiating case. The adducing of supporting considerations must be something that is not made in principle impossible under the circumstances: not *everything* can be disqualified as failing to count in this regard. All rational discussion presupposes an exchange of contentions, and it will not do in such a context simply to silence one of the parties by an extraneous act of *force majeure* that precludes him from the very outset from developing a case.

Accordingly, the situation must be such that there are always *some* considerations that are "allowed to count" towards building up an at least provisionally adequate case. Thus there must always be established ground rules specifying certain categories of contentions as endowed with evidential weight. It makes sense to speak of a "burden of proof" only in the context of established rules regarding the discharge of such a burden. In rational controversy, there must always be some impartially fixed common ground determining what is to count as evidence. This leads straightaway into the topic of *presumption*.

Presumption represents a way of filling in—at least *pro tem*—the gaps that may otherwise confront us at any stage of information. The French *Code civil* defines "presumptions" as: *"des conséquences qui la loi ou le magistrat tire d'un fait connu à un fait inconnu."* [7] A presumption indicates that in the absence of specific counterindications we are to accept how things "as a rule" are taken as standing, and it places the burden of proof upon the adversary's side. For example, there is, in

7. "Consequences drawn by the law or the magistrate from a known to an unknown fact." Bk. III, pt. iii, sect. iii, art. 1349.

most probative contexts, a standing presumption in favor of the usual, normal, customary course of things. The conception of burden of proof is correlative with that of a presumption. [The "presumption of innocence" can serve as a paradigm example here.]

In its legal setting, the conception of presumption has been explicated in the following terms:

> A presumption in the ordinary sense is an inference. . . . The subject of presumptions so far as they are mere inferences or arguments, belongs not to the law of evidence, or to law at all, but to rules of reasoning. But a legal presumption, or, as it is sometimes called, a presumption of law, as distinguished from presumptions of fact, is something more. It may be described, in [Sir James] Stephen's language, as "a rule of law that courts and judges shall draw a particular inference from a particular fact, or from particular evidence, unless and until the truth" (perhaps it would be better to say "soundness") "of the inference is disproved."[8]

Such a *presumptio juris* is a supposition relative to the known facts which, by legal prescription, is to stand until refuted.

Accordingly, presumptions, though possessed of significant probative weight, will in general be defeasible—i.e., subject to defeat in being overthrown by sufficiently weighty countervailing considerations. In its legal aspect, the matter has been expounded as follows:

> [A] presumption of validity . . . retains its force in general even if subject to exceptions in particular cases. It may not by itself state all the relevant considerations, but it says enough that the party charged should be made to explain the allegation or avoid responsibility; the plaintiff has given a reason why the defendant should be held liable, and thereby invites the defendant to provide a reason why, in this case, the presumption should not be made absolute. The presumption lends structure to the argument, but it does not foreclose its further development.[9]

The standing of a presumption is usually tentative and provisional, not absolute and final. A presumption only stands until the crucial issues that "remain to be seen" have been clarified, so that it is actu-

8. Sir Courtenay Ilbert, "Evidence," p. 15.
9. R. A. Epstein, "Pleadings and Presumptions," pp. 558–559.

ally seen whether the presumptive truth will in fact stand up once everything is said and done.[10] (Note that both a categorial thesis P and a conditional one of the type P/Q can have the status of a presumption.)

Specifically defeasible presumptions are closely interconnected with the conception of burden of proof:

> The effect of a presumption is to impute to certain facts or groups of facts a *prima facie* significance or operation, and thus, in legal proceedings, to throw upon the party against whom it works the duty of bringing forward evidence to meet it. Accordingly, the subject of presumption is intimately connected with the subject of burden of proof, and the same legal rule may be expressed in different forms, either as throwing the advantage of a presumption on one side, or as throwing the burden of proof on the other.[11]

In effect, a defeasible presumption is just the reverse of a burden of proof (of the "burden of further reply" variety). Whenever there is a "burden of proof" for establishing that P is so, the correlative defeasible presumption that not-P stands until the burden has been discharged definitively. Archbishop Whately has formulated the relationship at issue in the following terms:

> According to the most current use of the term, a "presumption" in favour of any supposition means, not (as has been sometimes er-

---

10. C. S. Peirce put the case for presumptions in a somewhat different way—as crucial to maintaining the line between sense and foolishness:

> There are minds to whom every prejudice, every presumption, seems unfair. It is easy to say what minds these are. They are those who never have known what it is to draw a well-grounded induction, and who imagine that other people's knowledge is as nebulous as their own. That all science rolls upon presumption (not of a formal but of a real kind) is no argument with them, because they cannot imagine that there is anything solid in human knowledge. These are the people who waste their time and money upon perpetual motions and other such rubbish. (*Collected Papers*, VI, 6.423; compare vol. II, 2.776–7.)

Peirce is very emphatic regarding the role of presumptions in scientific argumentation and adduces various examples, e.g., that the laws of nature operate in the unknown parts of space and time as in the known or that the universe is inherently indifferent to human values and does not on its own workings manifest any inclination towards being benevolent, just, wise, etc. As the above quotation shows, Peirce saw one key aspect of presumption to revolve about considerations regarding the *economics of inquiry*—i.e., as instruments of efficiency in saving time and money. On this section of his thought, see the author's paper "Peirce and the Economy of Research" in *Philosophy of Science* 43 (1976): 71–98.

11. R. A. Epstein, "Pleadings & Presumptions," pp. 558–559.

roneously imagined) a preponderance of probability in its favour, but such a *preoccupation* of the ground as implies that it must stand good till some sufficient reason is adduced against it; in short, that the *burden of proof* lies on the side of him who would dispute it.[12]

It is in just this sense, for example, that the "presumption of innocence" in favor of the accused is correlative with the burden of proof carried by the state in establishing his guilt.

In line with this idea, the circumstance that the burden of proof always rests with the party initially asserting a thesis leads to the view that there is automatically a *presumption against* any maintained thesis. But, of course, if the adducing of evidence in the dialectic of rational argumentation is to be possible at all, this circumstance must have its limits. Clearly, if the burden of proof inclined against *every* contention—if there were an automatic presumption of falsity against any contention whatsoever—it would become in principle impossible ever to provide a persuasive case. The rule that each contention needs evidential support through the adducing of further substantiating contentions cannot reasonably be made operative *ad indefinitum.*

In "accepting" a thesis as presumptively true one concedes it a probative status that is strictly provisional and *pro tem;* one does *not* say to it: "Others abide our question, thou art free."[13] There is no need here to invoke the idea of *unquestionable* theses, theses that are inherently uncontestable, certain, and irrefutable. To take this view would involve a misreading of the probative situation. It is to succumb to the tempting epistemological doctrine of foundationalism, that insists on the need for and ultimate primacy of absolutely certain, indefeasible, crystalline truths, totally beyond any possibility of invalidation. The search for such self-evident or protocol theses— inherently inviolate and yet informatively committal about the nature of the world—represents one of the great quixotic quests of modern

---

12. Richard Whately, *Elements of Rhetoric* (London and Oxford, 1828), Pt. I, Ch. III, sect. 2.

13. On the strictly empirical side, it is difficult to exaggerate the extent to which our processes of thought, communication, and argumentation in everyday life are subject to established presumptions and accepted plausibilities. This is an area that is only beginning to be subjected to sociological exploration. (See, for example, Harold Garfinkel, *Studies in Ethnomethodology* [Englewood Cliffs, 1967].) The pioneer work in the field is that of Alfred Schutz, *Der sinnhafte Aufbau der sozialen Welt* (Wien, 1932).

philosophy.[14] It deserves stress that an epistemic quest for categories of data that are *prima facie* acceptable (innocent until proven guilty, as it were) is altogether different from this quest for absolutely certain or totally self-evidencing theses which has characterized the mainstream of epistemological tradition from Descartes via Brentano to present-day writers such as Roderick Chisholm.

There is no need to embark on any such quest for absolute security in the context of present purposes. The probative requirements of disputational dialectic do not demand any category of irrefutable claims. All that is needed is that some theses inherently merit the "benefit of doubt" in that they are able to stand provisionally—i.e., until somehow undermined.[15]

In any essentially dialectical situation in which the idea of burden of proof figures, the very "rules of the game" remain inadequately defined until the issue of the nature, extent, and weight of the range of operative presumptions has been resolved in some suitable way. Burden of proof and presumption represent correlative conceptions inevitably coordinate with one another throughout the context of rational dialectic, because the recourse to presumptions affords the indispensable means by which a burden of proof can—at least provisionally—be discharged.

The idea of presumptive truth must thus play a pivotal role in all such various contexts where the notion of a "burden of proof" applies. The mechanism of presumption thus accomplishes a crucial epistemological task in the structure of rational argumentation. For there must clearly be some class of claims that are allowed at least *pro tem* to enter acceptably into the framework of argumentation, because if everything were contested then the process of inquiry could not progress at all.

---

14. For further discussion of this issue and for references to the literature, see the author's book on *The Coherence Theory of Truth* (Oxford, 1973).

15. Thus we can straightforwardly move from the *presumption* of P to the *assertion* of P if no difficulties arise for this step. (If difficulties *do* arise, rules of resolution are needed.) Analogously if we can move from the *assumption* of P to infer deductively the result Q, then we can straightforwardly assert the conditional theses $P \supset Q$ (by the "Deduction Theorem"). Assertion is, to be sure, the basic logical mode, and the other modes (*presumption, assumption,* etc.) are linked to it by characteristic logical principles. But to be the basic mode is not to be the *only* mode.

34

4. The locus of presumption

For a proposition to count as a presumption is something altogether different from its counting as a truth. A presumption is a plausible *pretender* to truth whose credentials may well prove insufficient, a runner in a race it may not win. The "acceptance" of a proposition as a presumptive truth is not *acceptance* at all but a highly provisional and conditional epistemic inclination towards it, an inclination that falls far short of outright commitment.

Our stance towards presumptions is unashamedly that of fairweather friends: we adhere to them when this involves no problems whatsoever, but abandon them at the onset of difficulties. But it is quite clear that such *loose* attachment to a presumption is by no means tantamount to no attachment at all.[16] However, a presumption stands secure only "until further notice," and it is perfectly possible that such notice might be forthcoming.

Against the claims of the senses or of memory automatically to afford us the truth pure and simple one can deploy all of the traditional arguments of the sceptics. And, in particular, we have before us the guidance of Descartes: "All that up to the present time I have accepted as most true and certain I have learned either from the senses or through the senses; but it is sometimes proved to me that these senses are deceptive, and it is wiser not to trust entirely to any thing by which we have once been deceived."[17] But, of course, such sceptical arguments in support of the potential untruthfulness of sensory data serve only to reemphasize their role as provisional truth-claims in our presumptive sense, rather than outright *truths* as such. (That potential fallibility proves actual falsehood and that these truth-candidates are in principle to be excluded from the realm of truth—in short that what is not known to be true is thereby known to be false—is something no sceptic has claimed to establish in even his

16. As I. Scheffler puts a similar point in the temporal context of a change of mind in the light of new information: "That a sentence may be given up at a later time does not mean that its present claim upon us may be blithely disregarded. The idea that once a statement is acknowledged as theoretically revisable, it can carry no cognitive weight at all, is no more plausible then the suggestion that a man loses his vote as soon as it is seen that the rules make it possible for him to be outvoted" (*Science and Subjectivity* [New York, 1967], p. 118).

17. René Descartes, *Meditations on First Philosophy,* No. I (tr. by R. M. Eaton).

most extravagant moments. And this being so, the door to truth-candidacy will remain open in the face of potential falsity.)[18]

To render this idea of *presumption* clearer and more vivid, it may be useful to survey its workings in the range of relevant cases.

(1) Law

Legal presumption (*praesumptio juris*) specifies an inference that is to be drawn from certain facts (or their absence): it indicates a conclusion which, by legal prescription, is to stand until duly set aside.

Such legal presumptions are sometimes irrefutable (as with the presumption that a child of less than seven years cannot commit a crime, or that the testimony of an incompetent [disqualified] witness is worthless). Such are the so-called "conclusive presumptions of law." More generally, however, the presumption is refutable, as with the "presumption of innocence" itself, the presumption that a person seven years lost is dead, the presumption that a child born or conceived in wedlock is legitimate, and the presumption that a document at least thirty years old is genuine. In all these cases the presumption can be defeated by appropriate evidence to the contrary.

(2) Disputation

In disputation (unlike law) all presumptions are, of course, of the defeasible sort. This is true not only of the fundamental presumption of falsity regarding freshly introduced theses, but also of the presumptions in favor of certain species of evidence, such as matters of "common knowledge" or the attest of suitable "authorities." (In both these cases one is dealing with presumptions of the evidential type.) Such refutable presumptions in effect serve to demarcate the rules of the evidential game with respect to the dialectic of disputation.

(3) Debate

Most debating textbooks seem to agree that in debate a presumption of truth must be accorded to what might be characterized as the cognitive *status quo:* the domain of what is "generally accepted"

18. The defeat of a defeasible presumption relates (in the case of a specific presumption of fact) to its upset by falsification in a particular instance rather than the distinction of the presumption rule as such. Of course, such a general rule or principle—the presumptive veracity of a reliable source, for example—can also be *invalidated* ("falsified" would be inappropriate). (For a further discussion of the relevant issues, see the author's *Methodological Pragmatism* [Oxford, 1976].)

and/or qualifies as "common knowledge."[19] A related case is that of the testimony of suitably qualified experts, which is also generally conceded as entitled to a presumption of truth. Or again, there is the familiar standing presumption in favor of the normal, usual, customary state of things. All such debating presumptions are clearly based on originals derived from disputation.

(4) Theory of knowledge

Presumption also plays an important part in the theory of knowledge itself. For example, a tradition in philosophical epistemology that reaches from the later Stoics and Academic Sceptics of antiquity to the British Idealists of the turn of the present century insists (not always *expressis verbis,* but in effect) on a presumption of truth in favor of the deliverances of memory and of the senses. Theses based on observation or recollection are to have the benefit of doubt, a presumption of truth in their favor—they are to stand unless significant counterindications are forthcoming. A comparable stance can—and should—be maintained towards the standard principles of evidential reasoning (and especially *inductive* reasoning) as well. A presumption of this character operates in favor of such inductive parameters as simplicity, uniformity, and the like.

5. Plausibility and presumption

Perhaps the single most important device for putting the idea of presumption to work is the conception of plausibility.[20] For plausibility can serve as the crucial determinant of where presumption resides. The basic principle here is that of the rule:

19. For presumptions, see pp. 70–74 of the French version of Ch. Perelman and L. Olbrechts-Tyteca, *The New Rhetoric: A Treatise on Argumentation* (Notre Dame, 1969; original French version: Paris, 1958).

20. Historically this goes back to the conception of "the reasonable" (*to eulogon*), as discussed in Greek antiquity by the Academic Sceptics. Carneades (c. 213–c. 128 B.C.) for one worked out a rather well-developed (nonprobabilistic) theory of plausibility as it relates to the deliverances of the senses, the testimony of witnesses, etc. For a helpful discussion of the relevant issues, see Charlotte L. Stough, *Greek Skepticism* (Berkeley and Los Angeles, 1969).

Presumption favors the most *plausible* of rival alternatives—when indeed there is one. This alternative will always stand until set aside (by the entry of another, yet more plausible, presumption).

The operation of this rule creates a key role for plausibility in the theory of reasoning and argumentation.[21] In the face of discordant considerations, one "plays safe" in one's cognitive involvements by endeavoring to maximize the plausibility levels achievable in the circumstances. Such an epistemic policy is closely analogous to the *prudential* principle of action—that of opting for the available alternative from which the least possible harm can result. Plausibility-tropism is an instrument of epistemic prudence.

To be sure, the plausibility of contentions is not the only route to presumptions. In a formal disputation, for example, a schedule of presumptions can be established by either a *negotiated agreement* arranged "internally" between the parties or an *imposed agreement* "externally" decreed by the determiner. Thus in addition to getting to presumption by the natural route of *plausibility assessment* one can also get there by the artificial route of *conventional agreement*. But this will work only within such contrived settings as formal disputation and law. In less contrived situations of debate and rational controversy, one must rely on the *natural* presumptions fixed by purely probative consideration of evidential weight and intrinsic plausibility. Plausibility accordingly emerges as a pivotal mechanism of *rational* (as opposed to *conventional*) dialectic.

The plausibility of a thesis will not be a measure of its *probability*—of how likely we deem it, or how surprised we would be to find it falsified. Rather, it reflects the prospects of its being fitted into our cognitive scheme of things in view of the standing of the sources or principles that vouch for its inclusion herein. The core of the present conception of plausibility is the notion of the extent of our cognitive inclination towards a proposition—of *the extent of its epistemic hold upon*

21. For an interesting analysis of presumptive and plausibilistic reasoning in mathematics and (to a lesser extent) the natural sciences, see George Polya's books *Introduction and Analogy in Mathematics* (Princeton, 1954) and *Patterns of Plausible Inference* (Princeton, 1954). Polya regards the patterns of plausible argumentation as defining the "rules of admissibility in scientific discussion" on strict analogy with the legal case, regarding such rules as needed because it is plain that not *anything* can qualify for introduction as probatively relevant.

us in the light of the credentials represented by the bases of its credibility. The key issue is that of how readily the thesis in view could make its peace within the overall framework of our cognitive commitments.

The standing of sources in point of authoritativeness affords one major entry point to plausibility. In this approach, a thesis is more or less plausible depending on the reliability of the sources that vouch for it—their entitlement to qualify as well-informed or otherwise in a position to make good claims to credibility. It is on this basis that "expert testimony" and "general agreement" (the consensus of men) come to count as conditions for plausibility.[22]

Again, the probative strength of confirming evidence could serve as yet another basis of plausibility. In this approach, the rival theses whose supporting case of substantiating evidence is the strongest is thereby the most plausible. Our evidential sources will clearly play a primary role.

The plausibility of contentions may, however, be based not on a thesis-warranting *source* but a thesis-warranting *principle.* Here inductive considerations may come prominently into play; in particular such warranting principles are the standard inductive desiderata: simplicity, uniformity, specificity, definiteness, determinativeness, "naturalness," etc. In such an approach one would say that the more simple, the more uniform, the more specific a thesis—either internally, of itself, or externally, in relation to some stipulated basis—the more emphatically this thesis is to count as plausible.

For example, the concept of *simplicity* affords a crucial entry point for plausibility considerations. The injunction "Other things being anything like equal, give precedence to simpler hypotheses vis-a-vis more complex ones" can reasonably be espoused as a procedural, regulative principle of presumption, rather a metaphysical claim as to "the simplicity of nature." On such an approach, we espouse not the Scholastic adage "Simplicity is the sign of truth" (*simplex sigilium veri*), but its cousin, the precept "Simplicity is the sign of plausibility" (*simplex sigilium plausibili*). In adopting this policy we shift the

---

22. This view of plausibility in terms of general acceptance either by the *consensus gentium* or by the experts ("the wise") was prominent in Aristotle's construction of the plausible (*endoxa*) in Book I of the *Topics.*

39

discussion from the plane of the constitutive/descriptive/ontological to that of the regulative/methodological/prescriptive.

Again, uniformity can also serve as a plausibilistic guide to reasoning. Thus consider the *Uniformity Principle:*

> In the absence of explicit counterindications, a thesis about unscrutinized cases which conforms to a patterned uniformity obtaining among the data at our disposal with respect to scrutinized cases—a uniformity that is in fact present throughout these data—is more plausible than any of its regularity-discordant contraries. Moreover, the more extensive this pattern-conformity, the more highly plausible the thesis.

This principle is tantamount to the thesis that when the initially given evidence exhibits a marked logical pattern, then pattern-concordant claims relative to this evidence are—*ceteris paribus*—to be evaluated as more plausible than pattern-discordant ones (and the more comprehensively pattern-accordant, the more highly plausible). This rule implements the guiding idea of the familiar practice of judging the plausibility of theories and theses on the basis of a "sufficiently close analogy" with other cases.[23] (The uniformity principle thus forges a special rule for *normality*—reference to "the usual course of things"—in plausibility assessment.)[24]

The situation may thus be summarized as follows. The natural

---

23. All this, of course, does not deal with question of the status of this rule itself and of the nature of its own justification. It is important in the present context to stress the *regulative* role of plausibilistic considerations. This now becomes a matter of *epistemic policy* ("Give priority to contentions which treat like cases alike") and not a metaphysically laden contention regarding the ontology of nature (as with the—blatantly false—descriptive claim "Nature is uniform"). The plausibilistic theory of inductive reasoning sees uniformity as a *regulative principle of epistemic policy* in grounding our choices, not as a *constitutive principle* of ontology. As a "regulative principle of epistemic policy" its status is *methodological*—and thus its justification is in the final analysis pragmatic. See the author's *Methodological Pragmatism* (Oxford, 1976).

24. See Ferdinand Gonseth, "La Notion du normal," *Dialectica* 3 (1947): 243–252. More generally, on the principles of plausible reasoning in the natural sciences see Norwood R. Hanson, *Patterns of Discovery* (Cambridge, 1958), and his influential 1961 paper "Is There a Logic of Discovery" in H. Feigl and G. Maxwell (eds.), *Current Issues in the Philosophy of Science,* Vol. I (New York, 1961). The work of Herbert A. Simon is an important development in this area: "Thinking by Computers" and "Scientific Discovery and the Psychology of Problem Solving" in R. G. Colodny (ed.), *Mind and Cosmos* (Pittsburgh, 1966).

bases of plausibility—the criteria operative in determining its presence in greater or lesser degree—fall primarily into three groups:

(1) *The standing of sources in point of authoritativeness.* On this principle, the plausibility of a thesis is a function of the reliability of the sources that vouch for it—their entitlement to qualify as well-informed or otherwise in a position to make good claims to credibility. It is on this basis that expert testimony and general agreement (the consensus of men) come to count as conditions for plausibility.

(2) *The probative strength of confirming evidence.* Of rival theses, that whose supporting case of substantiating evidence is the strongest is thereby the most plausible.

(3) *The tendency of principles of inductive systematization.* Other things being sufficiently equal, that one of rival theses is the most plausible which scores best in point of *simplicity,* in point of *regularity,* in point of *uniformity* (with other cases), in point of *normalcy,* and the like. The principles of presumption of this range correlate with the parameters of cognitive systematization.[25]

These three factors (source reliability, supportive evidence, and systematicity) are the prime criteria governing the assessment of plausibility in deliberations regarding the domain of empirical fact.

In general, the more plausible a thesis, the more smoothly it is consistent and consonant with the rest of our knowledge of the matters at issue. Ordinarily, the removal of a highly plausible thesis from the framework of cognitive commitments would cause a virtual earthquake; removal of a highly implausible one would cause scarcely a tremor; in between we have to do with varying degrees of readjustment and realignment. And in general, then, the closer its fit and the smoother its consonance with our cognitive commitments, the more highly plausible the thesis.[26]

25. All three of these principles of plausibility were operative in the protoconception of plausibility represented by Aristotle's theory of *endoxa* as developed in Book I of the *Topics.* For this embraced: (1) general acceptance by men at large or by the experts ("the wise"), (2) theses similar to these (or opposed to what is contrary to them), and (3) theses that have become established in cognitive disciplines (*kata technas*).

26. For a closer study of the notion of plausibility and its function in rational argumentation, see the author's *Plausible Reasoning* (Assen, 1976).

6. More on presumptions

The following objections might be made against the idea of defeasible presumptions. How can you speak of asserting a proposition merely as a presumption but not as a truth? If one is to assert (accept, maintain) the proposition in any way at all, does one not thereby assert (accept, maintain) it *to be true?* The answer here is simply a head-on denial, for there are different modes of acceptance. To maintain *P* as a presumption, as *potentially* or *presumptively* factual, is akin to maintaining *P* as *possible* or as *probable:* in no case are these contentions tantamount to maintaining the proposition as true. Putting a proposition forward as "possible" or "probable" commits one to claiming no more than that it is *"possibly* true" or *"probably* true." Similarly, to assert *P as a presumption* is to say no more than that *P* is *potentially* or *presumptively* true—that it is a truth-candidate—but does not say that *P* is *actually* true, that it is a truth. Acceptance does *not* lie along a one-dimensional spectrum which ranges from "uncertainty" to "certainty." There are not only *degrees* of acceptance but also *kinds* of acceptance. And *presumption* represents such a kind: it is *sui generis,* and not just an attenuated version of "acceptance as certain."

We do not intend the conception of a presumption to "open the floodgates" in an indiscriminate way. Not *everything* qualifies as a presumption: the concept is to have *some* probative bite. A presumption is not merely something that is "possibly true" or that is "true for all I know about the matter." To class a proposition as a presumption is to take a definite and committal position with respect to it, so as to say "I propose to accept it as true insofar as no difficulties arise from doing so."

There is thus a crucial difference between an *alleged* truth and a *presumptive* truth. For allegation is a *merely rhetorical* category: every contention that is advanced in discussion is "allegedly true"—that is, alleged-to-be-true. But presumption—that is, warranted presumption—is an *epistemic* category: only in certain special circumstances are contentions of a *sort* that they merit to be accepted as true provisionally, "until further notice." [27]

27. For further details regarding the important role of presumptions in the philosophical theory of knowledge, see the author's *Methodological Pragmatism* (Oxford, 1976).

7. The need for a termination process in rational controversy

A means for appraisal and evaluation is a fundamental precondition of rational controversy. Without the existence of objective *standards of adequacy,* rational controversy is inherently impossible. Argumentation is pointful as a rational process only if the extent to which a "good case" has been made out can be assessed in retrospect on a common, shared basis of judgment—be it agreed or imposed. Such adjudication calls for determining (at least provisionally) a "winning position." In providing an instrument essential to the "termination" (i.e., adjudication) of a rational debate, the ground rules of plausibility and presumption thus furnish a resource indispensable to the rationally appropriate conduct of the controversy. Without the guidance of an assessment mechanism for termination, the whole enterprise of disputing becomes futile. The machinery of plausibility and presumption thus serves to satisfy a key presupposition of the entire enterprise of rational dialectic.

The determiner of a debate is concerned to see which side has built up a better case (under the circumstances). There is a disparity here between conventional dialectics (in disputation, debate, and law) and natural dialectics (in rational controversy). In the former contexts the "determining" arbiter will follow certain purely conventional rules. (A legal trial is not concerned for the "real truth of the matter"—else why have categories of "inadmissable" evidence?—but for the making out of a legally proper case.) However, in the dialectic of rational controversy "natural" presumptions are the determining guide. Here a winning position is reached by the proponent when every initiating burden of proof has been discharged by him. This circumstance is realized when all the pertinent contentions have been carried back in the process of evidentially supportive argumentation to theses that stand in the status of presumptive truths not only in the first analysis, but in the final analysis as well, because no adequately weighty counterarguments against them are forthcoming within the dialectical context of the dispute.

Consider again the situation in formal disputation. A disputation, as we have seen, represents a dialectical alternation of claims and

43

challenges. Abstractly speaking, it would seem that the opponent is *bound* to win out. He simply counters any claim X with the automatic challenge of *quo warranto:* "But what right have you to maintain X?" And so we seem to be led down the primrose path of the endless and seemingly futile regress:

proponent	opponent
$T!$	$\dagger \sim T$
T/P & $!P$	$\dagger \sim P$
P/Q & $!Q$	$\dagger \sim Q$
Q/R & $!R$	$\dagger \sim R$
etc.	etc.

But the pivotal consideration here lies in the termination rule that the proponent is always striving to reach—and the opponent to prevent him from reaching—the safe ground of authenticated presumptions.

As a debate proceeds the natural tendency of the development is for the proponent to acquire more and more commitments. For example:

proponent	opponent
$!T$	$\dagger \sim T$
T/P & $!P$	$\sim T/(P$ & $Q)$ & $\dagger(P$ & $Q)$
$T/(P$ & Q & $R)$ & $!(P$ & Q & $R)$	

As argument moves further outwards along such a rationale-exfoliating tree, the proponent undertakes an ever more extensive and ramified series of commitments. But the plausibility of such a complex does not depend on the *number* of its components. It is important to recognize that the operative principle is one of a-chain-is-as-strong-as-its-weakest-link variety. The status of the *least* plausible commitment determines the status of the whole complex in which it figures.[28]

The proponent is in a "winning position" when *all* of his opponent's rebuttals—or at any rate those of them to which he has had a reasonable chance to reply when the point of termination is at hand—are covered by cogent counterarguments whose component premisses are *all* presumptive truths (or highly plausible theses). The opponent

---

28. Compare the discussion of the rules of plausibilistic inference in the author's *Plausible Reasoning* (Assen, 1976).

is in a "winning position" whenever *any one* of the proponent's contentions is left unprotected in point of adequate support through presumptive truths (or highly plausible theses). The disparity between the proponent and opponent in point of probative status is thus manifested by the fact that to realize a winning position the initiating proponent must be "protected" everywhere—and that a single "unprotected" position in his case leaves the victory in his opponent's hands. (As we have seen, this disparity is crucial for the operation of the conception of a *burden of proof* in this area of formal disputation or debate.) The *strength* of the protection at issue is determined by the "weakest link" principle. Such a termination rule in fact guides the whole *strategy* of procedure of the parties to the debating process. Each party to the debate strives to be in a winning position when the time arrives to terminate the debate.

The ground rules of presumption and plausibility accordingly furnish a key element governing the termination (adjudication) of disputation. Rational dialectic is possible only in the presence of an established methodology of probative assessment: not, to be sure, agreement on the *facts,* but on the machinery for the *evaluation of arguments*—on the probative mechanisms for the weighing of evidence, the appraisal of plausibility, etc. A shared procedure for the assessment of plausibility and the allocation of presumption thus emerges as a critical factor in dialectic—indeed, as one of the crucial presuppositions of rationality throughout the context of rational discussion.

3 Unilateral dialectics: a disputational model of inquiry

1. The shift from disputation to a cognitive methodology of inquiry

This chapter explores the doctrine that disputation and debate may be taken as a paradigmatic model for the general process of reasoning in the pursuit of truth, thus making the transition from rational *controversy* to rational *inquiry*. There is nothing new about this approach. Already the Socrates of Plato's *Theaetetus* conceived of inquiring thought as a discussion or dialogue that one carries on with oneself. Charles Sanders Peirce stands prominent among those many subsequent philosophers who held that discursive thought is always dialogical. But Hegel, of course, was the prime exponent of the conception that all genuine knowledge must be developed *dialectically*.

This historically prominent approach to inquiry as dialectical—as taking a form fundamentally akin to that of disputation—envisages a significant transformation of the ordinary disputational endeavor. The object now is *not to refute the contentions of an opposing spokesman, but to appraise the rational credentials of a thesis*. The process of reasoned exchange is reoriented from a bilateral adversary procedure of controversy and disputation to the unilateral enterprise of a "discussion" carried on with oneself, *in foro interno*, within a self-contained course of reflective thought.

This revised approach, accordingly, does not really reflect an ad-

46

versary proceeding, an "argument" in the sense of a dispute, but an "argument" in the other sense of the term—a course of probative reasoning. The aim here is not to win out over a rival *contender,* but to test a *contention* through the process of setting out the lines of reasoning by which these considerations are in turn met and countered. In such a unilateral reorientation of dialectic, dialectical methodology undergoes an evolutionary transformation from a methodology of *controversy* to one of *inquiry.* The transition from rational *debate* to rational *inquiry* is justified on the basis of the consideration that the aim of inquiry is to arrive at *defensible* results—i.e., claims which can be adequately supported in rational discussion.

In transforming the process of adversary dialectic into a unilateral one, an instrument for exploring the evidence is forged—a tool for clarifying the rationale of supporting considerations on whose basis a contention can be maintained. The function of this reoriented "dialectic" is to provide a *testing device* for the investigation of the probative or evidential grounding of theses. Dialectic now furnishes a mechanism for evaluating the supportive rationale of a thesis in the face of countervailing considerations: by scrutinizing the pros and cons that militate for or against a thesis, one is able to appraise the grounds that support it against its rivals. A *heuristic method of inquiry* is now at issue, one that develops a progressive sequence of considerations which does not set one contending *party* against another, but rather pits one *thesis* against its rivals, with the aim of refining its formulation, uncovering its basis of rational support, and assessing its relative weight.

One very important aspect of this transformation should be stressed. We must return to the difference between the *natural*—the "purely rational"—mechanisms for assessing presumption and plausibility and the merely *conventional* mechanisms, illustrated by certain essentially arbitrary and unreasoned devices of law (e.g., statutorily determined presumptions) and of disputation (e.g., conventionally canonical proof-tests), etc. All such merely artificial devices of probative procedure are abrogated in inquiry, where "pursuit of knowledge" is itself the only relevant task. Here the evidential rules of knowledge-oriented controversy apply without distorting constraints or restraints. When we make the transition from controversy to inquiry, it is purely rational controversy, with its natural (nonconventional) ground rules, that constitutes the paradigm.[1]

2. The platonic aspect of dialectic

These considerations point in particular towards that aspect of dialectic which lay at the forefront of Plato's concern. He insisted upon two fundamental ideas: (1) that a starting point for rational argumentation cannot be merely assumed or *postulated,* but must itself be *justified,* and (2) that the *modus operandi* of such a justification can be dialectical. Plato accordingly mooted the prospect of rising above a reliance on unreasoned first principles. He introduced the special device he called *"dialectic"* to overcome this dependence upon unquestioned axioms. It is worthwhile to see how he puts in his own terms:

> There remain geometry and those other allied studies which, as we said, do in some measure apprehend reality; but we observe that they cannot yield anything clearer than a dream-like vision of the real so long as they leave the assumptions they employ unquestioned and can give no account of them. If your premiss is something you do not really know and your conclusion and the intermediate steps are a tissue of things you do not really know, your reasoning may be consistent with itself, but how can it ever amount to knowledge? . . . So . . . the method of dialectic is the only one which takes this course, doing away with assumptions. . . . Dialectic will stand as the coping-stone of the whole structure; there is no other study that deserves to be put above it.[2]

Plato's writings do not detail in explicit terms the exact nature of this crucial enterprise of dialectic. Presumably we are to gain our insight into its nature not so much by way of *explanation* as by way of *example*—the example of Plato's own practice in the dialogues. And what emerges is pretty much the sort of dialectical process envisaged

1. Our primary concern here is with inquiry in the domain of contingent fact. But dialectics can provide a useful testing mechanism in the sphere of formal truth as well—and in particular in logic. For such a utilization of a dialectical model of logical proof, see Appendix 2 to Chapter Four.

2. *Republic,* Bk. VII, 533–534 (tr. F. M. Cornford).

in our present discussion: the comparative "cost-benefit" analysis of pros and cons of the proposed starting point in the face of its competing alternatives.

The general approach at issue is such that the axioms *validate* the consequences (by providing their inferential basis) and the consequences *vindicate* the axioms (in that intellectual cost-benefit comparisons show them to be relatively optimal in yielding desired results).

In such an approach, it is not necessary to acknowledge the need for any *indefensible* (as opposed to merely *undefended*) commitments in rational inquiry. Even the "first principles" ordinarily operative in rational inquiry—including such methodological parameters as simplicity, uniformity (coordination with other cases), etc.—can themselves be legitimated by dialectical means. We can analyze in detail what potential advantages and disadvantages their espousal has for the conduct of rational inquiry, weighing the pro and con considerations by procedures of the generally dialectical type.

3. Dialectic as evidential cost-benefit analysis

The disputational technique is clearly of value as an instrumentality of inquiry. In general—throughout all of inquiry—attempts at explanation and substantiation call for a supportive cost-benefit analysis of factors pro and con. One must balance the advantages that favor the claims at issue (in point of such factors as simplicity, explanatory power, reduction of merely seeming diversity, etc.) against the disadvantages (distortion, oversimplification, or loss in point of some aforementioned advantage). The technique of disputation affords a tailor-made device for the correlative assessment of pros and cons.

Approached from this general point of view, dialectic becomes a methodological instrument of inquiry for both discovery and exposition. It furnishes not only an instrument for mapping out the *static* probative rationale of support for a thesis, but also a *dynamic* mechanism of iterative deepening and refinement.

Let us see just how dialectic yields what is, in effect, a procedure for cost-benefit analysis in the cognitive sphere.

49

A closer analysis of this dialectical method of inquiry can usefully begin with the case in which a certain mooted "target" thesis T is to be assessed and evaluated in the face of its potential rivals T_1, T_2, etc. In such circumstances, the dialectic of counterargumentation will include two sorts of components:

(1) Challenges to the supporting grounds adduced for T, as when the challenge $\dagger\sim P$ is mounted against T/P & $!P$. Or again, consider the more subtle exchange taking roughly the following form:

PRO-*Phase*	CON-*Phase*
T/P & $!P$	$\sim T/(P$ & $Q)$ & $\dagger(P$ & $Q)$
$\begin{cases} T/(P$ & Q & $R)$ & $!(P$ & Q & $R) \\ \quad\quad\quad\text{or} \\ T/(P$ & $\sim Q)$ & $!(P$ & $\sim Q) \end{cases}$	

(2) Challenges to T itself in the interest of one or another of its rival alternatives, the T_i. Such challenges may take roughly the form:

PRO-*Phase*	CON-*Phase*
T/P & $!P$	$\sim T/(P$ & $T_i)$ & $\dagger(P$ & $T_i)$
$T/(P$ & $\sim T_i)$ & $!(P$ & $\sim T_i)$	$\dagger T_i$
$\sim T_i/K$ & $!K$	

In cases of the former sort, there is an oblique challenge to a thesis T through an attack on one of its purported supporting grounds (viz., P)—either directly, or by means of the observation that this ground will not serve its intended purpose, given the complicating presence of some countervailing consideration. In cases of the latter sort, a direct challenge to T itself is made in the name of one of its rivals. The former cases call for essentially defensive moves by the "proponent" to support his thesis in the light of counterconsiderations. The latter cases involve essentially offensive moves, by which the "proponent" attacks the counterconsiderations adduced by his "opponent."

Situations of the type set out in the exchange under point (1) are particularly interesting. Note that the pro-phase contention does *not* gainsay the con-phase contention $\sim T/(P$ & $Q)$. Rather, by introducing the added qualification R, thus shifting the ground from Q to

Q & R, the "proponent" has shown how his thesis T is preserved—or, in Hegelian terminology, *aufgehoben* ("sublated")—in the face of a counterconsideration which has been (appropriately) adduced on behalf of T's contradictory. Note that in both cases here the "proponent" has augmented his position through an extension, by moving from P alone as supporting consideration for T to the ampler and more fully refined basis P & Q & R (or else to P & $\sim Q$). Such a shift introduces an element of further sophistication in the development of the probative rationale—a move that becomes clearly needed once the prospect $\sim T/(P$ & $Q)$ is posed. Initially the pro-line of thought inclined to ground T on P alone, but the insufficiency of this grounding is recognized and the need for its supplementation taken into account. The process is thus designed to elicit the development of an increasingly adequate probative rationale. This aspect of the matter is particularly clear in the case of an exchange of the following sort:

PRO-*Phase*	CON-*Phase*
P	$\sim P/Q$ & $\dagger Q$
$P/(Q$ & $R)$ & $!(Q$ & $R)$	$\sim P/(Q$ & R & $S)$ & $\dagger(Q$ & R & $S)$
$P/(Q$ & R & S & $T)$ & $!(Q$ & R & S & $T)$	

What does such a dialectical model of cognitive inquiry accomplish? What is the product of its operation?

What it provides is an instrument for probing and evaluating pro factors and the con factors and for setting them out systematically—putting them in apposition and setting them off against one another.

On this basis the function of dialectic is, as presently conceived, essentially that of a *probative* cost-benefit analysis that weighs the pros and cons of adopting a thesis in the face of its alternatives. It sets out the pro considerations and the con considerations that militate for and against the contention at issue.[3] The dialectical process affords an instrument for answering such questions as: What considerations speak

---

3. The considerations operative here are not only those of the *evidential* sort, but can also include *systematic* considerations (e.g., overall uniformity and simplicity). Both the evidential benefits (or costs) *to* a thesis and the systematic benefits (or costs) *of* a thesis can function in the cost-benefit analysis at issue.

for acceptance of a thesis and what considerations against it? To what extent do these offset one another?[4]

4. A digression on written exposition

The probative processes at issue in such unilateral dialectic can be seen at work particularly vividly in the case of written exposition. Writing of persuasive intent is closely comparable to disputation. The author is cast in the role of a proponent, and his reader is cast in the dual roles of sceptical opponent and determiner (both as opposing attorney and as judge, so to speak). Reasoning in written exposition can and should be regarded as *argumentation* aimed at winning over an opponent: in both of the senses of "winning over," namely *defeating* the objections he made in his role as opponent, and *persuading or convincing* him in his role as adjudicative determiner. (It warrants incidental remark that this probative character of written exposition is particularly striking in the case of philosophy, where books very commonly have a heavily dialectical aspect. Examples include the dialogues of Plato, Spinoza's procedure of *more geometrico* demonstration with its interjection of argumentative *scholia,* or the quasi-judicial manner of argumentation encountered in authors like Berkeley and Hume.)

A particularly vivid, if somewhat stylized, example of this expository process is the medieval scholastic treatise, which tended to take on a structure particularly closely akin to that of a disputation. It ex-

---

4. These considerations highlight the difference between the present approach to dialectic and that of Hegel. For Hegel, dialectic addresses itself primarily to *concepts* ("terms") and is concerned to improve their *articulation,* whereas our present dialectic addresses itself primarily to *propositions* ("theses") and is concerned to improve their *substantiation.* To be sure, these two enterprises are not unrelated—particularly since *distinction* (or "division") with respect to concepts is one of the prime procedures of propositional disputation. But the overall procedures are sufficiently distinct to mark a significant difference between the rhetorical (disputational) form of the present approach to dialectic and the concept-analytical (hermeneutic) version of the Hegelian approach. On this issue of the historically different versions of dialectic, see the useful minihistory of Karl Dürr, "Die Entwicklung der Dialektik von Platon bis Hegel," *Dialectica* 1 (1947): 45–62.

plicitly included the whole disputational paraphernalia of thesis and denial, objections and replies, counterobjections and counterreplies. At the height of its development the scholastic treatise was, to all intents and purposes, a disputation transposed into literary form.

The author, as the proponent, is thus subject to the dialectical disabilities that ordinarily go with this role. The burden of proof rests on his side: it is incumbent on him to make out a case for any positive thesis he advances as a contention. Dialectic becomes a probative tool, a method for sifting the evidence so as to set it out *systematically*, in a rationally organized structure that exhibits the fabric of supporting reasons.

These considerations affect both the form and the content of written exposition of persuasive intent. The product of reasoned inquiry is—or ought to be—not merely disjointed bits and pieces of knowledge, but a *system* of knowledge. For such inquiry seeks to provide an architechtonically organized structure of contentions and grounds—of thesis and reason-to-maintain-thesis and reason-to-maintain-reason, etc. (not indefinitely, to be sure, but as long as is necessary or desirable). Only such a structured complex of grounded theses and grounding considerations deserves to be characterized as a *rationale*. The production of such a rationale for maintained theses—and the correlative identification of theses for which such a rationale can be constructed—is surely the pivotal function of rational inquiry. And dialectic, as we have construed it, is a natural and efficient means towards the realization of this end of systematic exposition.

5. The isomorphism of the disputational and probative versions of dialectic

The preceding considerations indicate that the general process of dialectic can assume two rather distinct forms whose structure is altogether parallel. In each instance, what is at issue is a process which proceeds by way of a fundamentally cyclic pattern of sequential development:

(1) As an adversary procedure in disputation, taking the form: initial defense of thesis → counterargument (antithesis)→ return to the starting point by an improved defense of thesis that encompasses (bypasses or overcomes) the counterargument (synthesis).

(2) As a methodology for probative testing in inquiry, taking the form: tentatively adopting a probative position → critique in the light of counterconsiderations → return to the starting point by the formulation of an improved position. (Such a process can take either a purely *intellectual* or an actually *empirical* form, that is, it can either take the form of a testing by *supportive grounds* in the purely rational domain, or else, in the empirical sciences, a testing by *observational evidence or actual experimental trial*.)

On both sides one encounters a fundamental sameness of structure. For either way the dialectical process amounts to one and the same pattern of cyclical feedback, depicted in Figure 4.

Figure 4
THE COMMON STRUCTURE OF DISPUTATION AND PROBATIVE INQUIRY

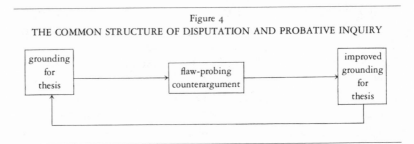

We simply have two distinguishable, but closely analogous, modes of cognitive advance in the face of a process of "trial" aiming at the detection of flaws. Such a cycle makes for the successive development by thesis-reformulation and rationale-sophistication of a closer and closer fit between a thesis—as duly refined and reformulated—and the supportive considerations that provide its warranting grounds. As this analysis shows, both processes alike deal with the issue of sequential improvements called for by "standing up to a challenge" through an exposure to counterarguments. The basic mission is the same on either side: the iterative deepening of a probative rationale.[5] On this perspective, dialectical rationality is the very paradigm of rationality in general.

6. The issue of evaluation and assessment

One crucial aspect of the analogy between disputation and inquiry merits closer attention. This is the pivotal issue of adjudication—of the assessment that enters into the "determination" of a disputation or the evaluation of a probative case. (After all, it would be pointless to set out on the venture if there were no reasonable prospect of reaching its end.)

Now to be in a position to evaluate a probative case requires not only that we be able to evaluate the relational moves of argumentation or grounding (say those of the sort we have depicted as taking the form X/Y), but also that we must be able to evaluate the grounds themselves. To be in a position to "determine" on which side of the dispute the better case lies, one must have means of assessing the merits and demerits of undefended commitments—commitments that are not necessarily indefensible but remain undefended at this stage. Throughout rational controversy, such undefended commitments will and must always play a part in the defense of others, and their appraisal is a crucial—nay, indispensable—component of the rational adjudication of a dialectical venture.

5. Note that the Popperian model of science as a cycle of conjecture and refutation conforms to this same probative pattern:

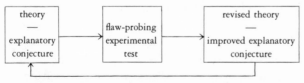

The characteristic feature of this special case of empirical science is that the step of "flaw-probing counterargument" here tends to become specifically experimental. For a vivid picture of Popperian methodology in the light of a dialectical perspective of consideration see Hans Albert, *Traktat über kritische Vernunft* (Tübingen, 1968).

What one must do in rational inquiry is pull oneself up by one's own bootstraps. We begin by provisionally accepting certain theses whose initial status is not that of certified truths at all, but merely that of plausible postulations, whose role in inquiry is (at this stage) one of regulative facilitation. Eventually these are retrovalidated (retrospectively revalidated) by the results of that inquiry. At *that* stage their epistemic status—though not their *content*—changes. *In the first instance* these presumptions have a merely provisional and regulative standing, though in the final instance they attain a suitable degree of factual-constitutive substantiation.

Through their use as probative devices of factual inquiry, presumptions come to serve as components of an input-output process of the type pictured in Figure 5.

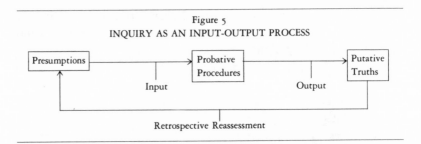

Figure 5
INQUIRY AS AN INPUT-OUTPUT PROCESS

An inquiry procedure having this overall structure escapes the vitiating cycle of basing truth-claims solely upon previously established claims and does so without appeal to a problematic category of self-certifying truths.

The viability of our bases of plausibility and presumption is a crucial requisite of dialectical rationality. But in inquiry this legitimacy cannot be guaranteed *a priori* on the basis of the "general principles" of the matter. It is something which only emerges *ex post facto* in the course of trial and error. The logical structure of this justificatory process incorporates a feedback loop leading from the truths validated by the inquiry procedure back to the initial "merely presumptive" truths, so that the appropriateness of the initial, tentative, merely plausible presumptions can be reassessed. This points towards a cyclic process of revalidation and cognitive upgrading in the course

56

of which presumptive theses used as inputs for the inquiry procedure come to acquire by gradual stages an enhanced epistemic status.

Of course, things need not always go smoothly for presumptions. For one thing this process clearly makes retrospective reevaluation possible: the outputs can bite the input-providing hand that feeds them and eventually dismiss some inputs as false. An initial presumption may well drop by the wayside in the long run. It is only normal and to be expected that this should happen, given the merely tentative probative nature of presumptions. But if it happens systematically rather than sporadically—if presumptions *generally* turn out false in this light of hindsight—then something has gone seriously amiss. (Yet one can, without problems, invalidate an entire source that has provided a basis of presumptions, as, for example, abandonment of the longstanding practice of giving probative weight to dreams, omens, signs, portents, etc.)

One sometimes hears it suggested that in rational inquiry one must put all prejudgments, all cognitive "prejudices" regarding plausibility and presumption aside. This is simply wrong. It is clear that meaningful argument cannot proceed *in vacuo*. As Peirce rightly insisted, in inquiry we must always begin from where we are—with an established, "in place" criteriology of probative procedure, preeminently including the mechanisms of plausibility and presumption. To be sure, these inputs of inquiry are themselves not indifferent to its results—they are subject to criticism and revision and relate to how things stand in the *first* rather than in the *final* analysis. But the fact of their corrigibility does not contravene their essentiality to the enterprise.

Dialectical *inquiry* thus needs standards of presumption and plausibility every bit as much as an adversary process of disputation does— in both cases alike, it is essential to the pointfulness of the enterprise to have rules of termination. For only by their means can one assess the adequacy of the rationale of supporting considerations developed in the course of an inquiry.

The dialectical model of rational inquiry accordingly calls for a set of suitable standards for assessing the plausibility or acceptability of the presumptions relied on in argumentation. The conceptions of plausibility and presumption must be allotted an indispensable role also in the "unilateral dialectics" of inquiry. The parallelism of function indicates a parallelism of process. The standards and criteria of rational dialectic will have to operate in essentially the same way in both public controversy and private inquiry. This important point needs closer scrutiny.

7. The probative isomorphism of controversy and inquiry

The search for a persuasively solid rationale that is characteristic of disputation is *isomorphic*—structurally identical—with the search for an evidentially sound rationale in probative inquiry. Such a parallelism between the structure of disputation and that of probative inquiry is not, or should not be, surprising. For the *structural* equivalence at issue roots in an unmistakable *functional* equivalence: that of building up *a good case* for the thesis at issue. Such a case is "good" by being *convincing*. And it is immaterial here whether it is *someone else* (say "the judicious arbiter" who determines a dispute) that *is* to be convinced in disputation, or *oneself* that *ought* to be convinced in inquiry. The basic issue is the same on both sides—that of building up a probatively sound argument.

The concept of a cogent argument or good reason is thus altogether *invariant* whether it is a matter of one's trying to convince *another* (in debate) or *oneself* (in rational inquiry). The concepts of reason and ground are impersonal and objective. There may not be such a thing as a *private* language, but there is certainly no such thing as an idiosyncratic canon of standards of reasoning—a *private logic*. The very phrase is a contradiction in terms. The crucial and basic question is not "How do I convince myself that X is so?" but "How do we convince one another of it?"[6] (The egocentric perspective of modern epistemology since Descartes has done much damage.) The business of giving—or probing for—a good reason for accepting a thesis will

---

6. As Aristotle saw, endeavoring to construct a convincing case for oneself is something secondary, a mere training device for the really important business of convincing others. (See *Topics*, 163b5.)

have to be the same in the context of personal inquiry as in public controversy.

Somebody might perhaps object as follows:

> You are overlooking the crucial role of *sense perception* and *memory* in factual inquiry. These, after all, are inescapably subjective processes. Does not the dialectical—i.e., *discursive*—model of cognitive warranting destroy the claims of perception and memory as source of knowledge?

Not at all. On the present approach, the role of the "directly evident" in perception, memory, etc., is not regarded as a direct "source of *knowledge*" but rather as a locus of *presumption* (exactly as with the Academic Sceptics). The claim "I see it" is not immediately knowledge-validating, but only ultimately so in the absence of counterindications. Thus consider the exchange: "There is a sundial in the quad"; "How do you know?" "I see it." This only indicates adequate warrant for the knowledge-claim if the matter *ends* there, so that the presumption at issue becomes final. If further exchanges indicate that (for example) no one else sees the sundial, then while the initial interlocutor may still persist in maintaining "I 'see' [i.e., take myself to be seeing] a sundial in the quad," the objective claim "There *is* a sundial in the quad" is certainly not adequately validated as an item of factual knowledge.

But the argument can be pressed a step further:

> You say that a cogent argument is something altogether invariant between one's trying to convince *another* (in debate) or *oneself* (in rational inquiry). How does this square with the fact that I cannot convince *you* that the cat is on the mat by taking a good look at the mat myself? Surely perception and memory introduce an essential difference between controversy and inquiry.

But this objection is misguided. Consider an analogy: a friend of mine, who was witness to some occurrence, will only give information about it to me and not to you (i.e., you only have access to the information obliquely, through me). Surely this circumstance is probatively quite irrelevant. The source of data only matters insofar as their significance is concerned. And all the probative issues relating to the *reliability* of the source, his *competence* as observer, the *evidential bearing* of his declaration, etc., are matters of public property. That

59

only a certain individual may have access to the declarations of a certain source is beside the point of the entire issue of the probative weight and bearing of the declarations of this source, all of which are fundamentally public and discursive issues.

The root issue in probative rationality is that of "building up a good case" to enlist the conviction of one's fellows. Accordingly, probative standards are person-indifferent; they are inherently public and communal. The testing standards of convincingness relate not to what convinces me or you as idiosyncratic individuals, but to what is convincing in general. It is thus only natural that the process of argumentation in rational inquiry as carried on in the precincts of a single mind should ultimately have to conform to that of persuasive dialectic in discussion and controversy. The very conception of duly validated knowledge-claims relates to publicly established and interpersonally operative standards. To abandon these in favor of some putatively personalized standards of inquiry—withdrawing to the use of private criteria, however well intentioned—is to secede from the community of rational reasoners and to abandon the project of rationality as such.

4 Facets of "dialectical logic"

1. Introduction

Theoreticians since Hegel's day who concern themselves with the "logic" of dialectics have maintained various theses that seem both bizarre and patently untenable from the perspective of orthodox logical theory. Accordingly, a wide and seemingly unbridgeable gulf has opened up between standard logicians and dialectical theorists.[1] The task of this chapter is to survey some of these apparently paradoxical principles of "dialectical logic."[2]

A word on objectives is in order. We are not here concerned with Hegel exegesis nor with the "rational reconstruction" of a Hegelian (i.e., Hegel-reminiscent) position. The issue before us is rather that posed by logicians in the Marxist tradition who have endeavored to construct a specifically *dialectical* logic. We confront the question: how do the present deliberations regarding disputational dialectic

---

1. This gulf manifests itself in the virtually ubiquitous tendency for standard logicians to dismiss dialectics:

   ". . . there is, obviously, no such thing as 'dialectical logic.' " (I. M. Bochenski, "Soviet Logic," *Studies in Soviet Thought* 1 [1961]: 29–38.)

   [Dialectical logic] seems a desperate, and hopeless, quibble . . . resulting from the impossible attempt to uphold simultaneously the principles of formal logic and of dialectic. (G. L. Kline, in a review of articles in *Voprosy filosofii* treating the relationship of formal logic and dialectical logic, *The Journal of Symbolic Logic* 18 [1958]: 83–86.)

   . . . it is the author's prediction that Soviet logic will not develop fruitfully or successfully, and for this three principal reasons are alleged: lack of freedom for creative thought, extreme Russian nationalism, and incompatibility of logic and dialectic. (Alonzo Church in a review of A. Philipov's *Logic and Dialectic in the Soviet Union, The Journal of Symbolic Logic* 18 [1958]: 272–273.)

2. However, dialectical—and specifically disputational—techniques can be used as a mechanism for the construction of logic itself (even in its "classical" form). For attempts along these lines, see Appendix 2 to this chapter.

61

bear on the dispute between the old (formal) vs. the new (dialectical) logic? And it will emerge that the present considerations actually leave room for accommodating dialectical principles within the setting of the traditional logic. The seemingly anomalous theses that have preoccupied dialectical logicians can be given a relatively natural and unproblematic interpretation within the present disputational approach to dialectics.

2. The tolerance of selfcontradiction: abandoning the law of contradiction

Logic—orthodox logic, the logic of the logicians since Aristotle's day—is irrevocably committed to the exclusion of contradictions. This stance is enshrined in the "Law of Contradiction" to the effect that P and $\sim P$ cannot both be maintained together, that one or the other of them must always be abandoned.

Now this is not so in the context of unilaterally dialectical reasoning. In bilateral controversy, to be sure, there is a division of labor— in general one party takes a pro stance towards a thesis, the other a con stance. But in the fusion of adversary disputation into a unilateral dialectic of inquiry, it may eventuate that one and the same party espouses both P and $\sim P$, assuming—within the setting of one and the same discussion—*both* a positive *and* a negative inclination towards the thesis P. We might, for example, encounter the sequence:

pro	con
P/Q & $!Q$	$\sim P/(Q$ & $R)$ & $\dagger(Q$ & $R)$

The pro phase argues for the contention that P, the anti phase supports (or strongly insinuates) that $\sim P$. Both P and $\sim P$ are advocated at different stages or phases (Hegelian "moments") of one synoptically coherent investigation.[3]

3. Thus in motivating his system of "dialectical" logic, the Polish logician S. Jaskowski writes:

It suffices . . . to deduce consequences from several hypotheses that are inconsistent with

Now ordinarily there may well be considerable justification for the "charge of inconsistency" that runs: "But look, you cannot (reasonably and sensibly) argue both for P and for $\sim P$." However, in the context of a dialectically probative investigation this seemingly obnoxious practice makes perfectly good sense. For this abridgment of the Law of Contradiction lies deep in the nature of rational controversy as a mode of argumentation that is less than *totally* conclusive. We know that in the case of *deductively valid* arguments one cannot reason from true premises to mutually inconsistent conclusions by the principles of classical deductive logic. But this is not so in subdeductive argumentation. Here it becomes entirely possible—in theory, at any rate—to build up powerfully convincing arguments for mutually inconsistent conclusions. When the premises at our disposal are merely plausible or probable (rather than categorically true) and the modes of inference we use are ampliative and inductively strong (rather than logically airtight), the prospect of building up cogent arguments on the one side for P and on the other for $\sim P$ is wide open.

Thus within the setting of such a dialectical process there arises not quite an abandonment of the Law of Contradiction, but at least a drastic qualification of it. For the abandonment is not total—the maintenance of $(P \ \& \ \sim P)/Q$ or the combination of P/Q with $\sim P/Q$ still remain blocked on strictly logical grounds.[4] But the maintenance both of P (relative to a consistent basis Q) and of $\sim P$ (relative to Q *together with something else that is altogether compatible with it*) is definitely a possibility. In certain circumstances one may well defend both P and $\sim P$—not, perhaps, "in one and the same beneath," but certainly in successive ones. And so when we make our cognitive posits subject to the guidance of "the best available reasons," we may well find ourselves having to "hedge our bets" through an endorsement of initially contradictory theses.

one another in order to change the nature of the theses, that shall no longer reflect a uniform opinion. The same happens if the theses advanced by several participants in a discourse are combined into a single system. . . . . (*Studia Logica* 28 [1969]: 149.)
This motivation in terms of a combining of the contributions of different discussants is clearly similar to our present disputational approach.

4. For the endeavors of modern logicians to devise systems of logic that do actually abandon the Law of Contradiction, see Appendix 1 to this chapter.

3. Curtailing the consequences of inconsistency: abandoning "ex falso quodlibet"

The now usual construction of the medieval principle *ex falso quodlibet* is as maintaining that anything whatsoever follows from the conjoining of incompatible theses—those whose conjunction is *logically* false. In the light of the preceding considerations, this principle too must clearly be abandoned—or at any rate curtailed—in the framework of dialectics. If we wish to be in a position to incline both to P and to $\sim P$, then we cannot adopt the stance that once a contradiction occurs—once P and $\sim P$ are both acknowledged—then anything whatsoever follows.[5]

To be sure, we cannot ever have (under any consistently maintainable and logically viable condition Q) that both P/Q and $\sim P/Q$. For then Q would indeed produce a logical anomaly. But we can certainly have it that both P/Q and $\sim P/(Q \ \& \ R)$. The circumstance that, despite the obtaining of P/Q, the *further* addition of R would lead to the contradictory of P, does not mean that this circumstance (viz., $Q \ \& \ R$) need produce a logical armageddon in which anything goes. In maintaining P/Q, we are not logically constrained thereby to abandon $\sim P/(Q \ \& \ R)$. (To be sure, in *deductive* logic the maintenance of $Q \vdash P$ forces an abandonment of $(Q \ \& \ R) \vdash \sim P$—*conjunctive qualifications* cannot undo *deductive* commitments. But this only goes to show the slash relationship of probatively evidential support is decisively different from the consequence relationship of logical entailment.

4. Potential indeterminacy: abandoning the law of excluded middle

Orthodox logic has it that any (well-defined) thesis is either true or false. The truth-status of theses is determinate in any realizable circumstance or condition. No matter what "the real world" may ul-

---

5. A dialectical logician must thus favor those increasingly common relevant logics that reject the thesis $(p \ \& \ \sim p) \rightarrow q$. On this issue, see A. R. Anderson and N. D. Belnap, Jr., *Entailment* (Princeton, 1975).

timately prove to be like, we shall have it either that P or else that $\sim P$. *Tertium non datur,* "there is no third possibility"—so states the Law of Bivalence of orthodox logic. The question "Is P the case or is it not?" here admits only two answers: "Yes, we have it that P" and "No, we have it that $\sim P$."

Orthodox logic accordingly looks towards "how the world really is"—it takes an orthodox ontological perspective, subject to the idea that "a real world" is thesis-decisive in its structure and cannot "fail to make up its mind" (so to speak) as to whether or not P is the case. On such an ontologically geared perspective, a world, be it real or merely really possible, must (so it is generally held) be fully determinate and "come down on one side or the other" with respect to every thesis P.

In *epistemic* logic, on the other hand, where our concern is with the world *as we know it* rather than the world *as it is,* a third possibility opens up. One may perfectly well be so circumstanced as to know neither that P is the case nor that $\sim P$ is.

Now in this regard, the situation in dialectic as we presently construe it must be assimilated to that of epistemic logic. For dialectic is *perspectival*—its key procedure is to maintain theses relative to grounding considerations via a probative relationship of the type: X/Y. And it may well eventuate that, in a given evidential situation Q, we hall have *neither P/Q nor $\sim P/Q$.* For Q may well fail to speak with adequate decisiveness on behalf either of P or of $\sim P$. Specifically, we may well find ourselves so circumstanced that, in the final analysis:

(1) We cannot maintain P/Q because we could only defensibly maintain $P/(Q \& R)$

(2) We cannot maintain $\sim P/Q$ because we could only defensibly maintain $\sim P/(Q \& S)$

It can thus happen under suitable dialectical conditions that a thesis can neither be maintained-to-be-true nor yet maintained-to-be-false. In this sense one must recognize the need to open up middle ground by rejecting the Law of Excluded Middle. (To be sure, in the specific form $(P \text{ v } \sim P)/Q$ the excluded-middle principle remains an unproblematic truism.)

The failure of excluded middle is, however, of quite a different character than that of the Law of Contradiction. For the Law of Excluded Middle fails in dialectics owing to the prospect of an informational indeterminacy or underdetermination, while the Law of Contradiction fails, not because the evidence at our disposal is too weak, but becaue the evidence is too strong, and includes elements that militate for P and offsetting elements that militate for $\sim P$ as well.

5. Constructive negation: abandoning the law of double negation

Negation in orthodox logic is no less positive a process than assertion: the negation of P just is the assertion of the contradictory $\sim P$. Negation is simply *displacement:* we no longer take our stance at P, but outside it. Negation is not *erasure:* it does not just take away, but *substitutes* something else—the contradictory denial of a thesis. Negation is thus a matter of *replacement by a denial:* to negate P is to assert $\sim P$. Its bearing is not agnostic but atheistic, so to speak.

In dialectic, however, negation may prove to be not just a matter of displacement, but of *refinement.* When P/Q is succeeded by $\sim P/(Q \,\&\, R)$, there is not just the displacement of the transition from P to $\sim P$, but also the refinement (amplification, improvement) of the transition from Q to $(Q \,\&\, R)$.

Thus a dialectical exchange like

pro	con
$P/Q \,\&\, !Q$ $\left\{ \begin{array}{c} P/(Q \,\&\, R \,\&\, S) \,\&\, !(Q \,\&\, R \,\&\, S) \\ \text{or} \\ (P/(Q \,\&\, \sim R) \,\&\, !(Q \,\&\, \sim R) \end{array} \right.$	$\sim P/(Q \,\&\, R) \,\&\, \dagger(Q \,\&\, R)$

does not consist of *purely* negative or contradictory countermoves: it advances the discussion and shifts the issue onto a more sophisticated ground.

This scenario can yield a dialectical process of somewhat Hegelian aspect. For consider the movement through a sequence of successive appraisals of the target thesis. At the first stage we have a picture of the probative situation such that a certain thesis is substantiated (i.e., we have T/P). At the second stage further scrutiny may reveal that this picture of the situation is inadequate or incorrect: a closer reading of the probative situation is counterindicative towards T (i.e., we have $\sim T/(P\ \&\ Q)$). Subsequently a third stage is reached in which the limitations of the second-stage standpoint come to light, and the justification for the first-stage picture is restored in a duly corrected form (i.e., we have $T/(P\ \&\ Q\ \&\ R)$). We reach a position of the sort where the argument for T is *aufgehoben* in the Hegelian sense of the term: it is cancelled but yet preserved. The cyclic structure of this dialectical process is as in Figure 6. In such a sequence, the negation not so much annihilates its target as serves to provide a stimulus and occasion for its sophistication and elaboration.

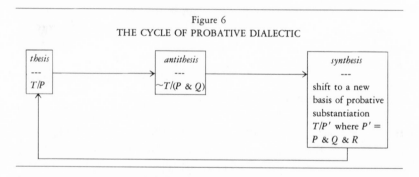

Figure 6
THE CYCLE OF PROBATIVE DIALECTIC

A series of exchanges of the form

$$P/Q \text{ to } \sim P/(Q\ \&\ R) \text{ to } \begin{cases} P/(Q\ \&\ \sim R) \\ P/(Q\ \&\ R\ \&\ S) \end{cases}$$

thus does not represent a *circle* but a constructive *advance*. We return to the starting point (viz., the maintenance of P given Q), but at a higher level of sophistication. The basic contention (viz., that P) is the same, but its grounding relative to Q has become more sophisticated (through the adjoining of $\sim R$ or of R & S). The underlying movement is not that of a *circle* but that of a *spiral*.

6. Conclusion

The situation in dialectical reasoning seemingly departs from that in orthodox logic in various ways. But *none of these anomalies is actually paradoxical*—at any rate in the approach to the issue adopted here. They represent *differences* from the situation that obtains in deductive logic, but not *violations* of it. Perfectly good "logical" sense can be made of these so-called "departures from orthodox logic" in the context of disputational dialectic. The various apparently divergent theses can all be maintained in a perfectly reasonable way: they are logically innocuous and perfectly understandable.

A striking conclusion thus emerges when our present theory of dialectical inconsistency is placed against the background of logical considerations. For *the present approach*—as we have seen—*dispenses entirely with any need to modify the principles of classical logic.* Despite its attempt to provide for the traditional principles of "dialectical" reasoning, nevertheless, at the crucial level of logical theory, our theory requires no innovations or renovations whatsoever.

Thus while the rules of "dialectical logic" in disputation depart from those encountered in standard logic, they do not thereby violate or contradict them. Given different phenomena we can expect different rules. The seeming anomaly of the departures of dialectical from logical procedures disappears in the face of the consideration that dialectical principles, at any rate *as construed in the context of traditional disputational dialectic,* nowise involve any actual transgression of orthodox logical principles.

Appendix 1
Recent ventures in inconsistency-tolerant logics

The rather orthodox upshot of the preceding considerations regarding logical ramifications of the dialectical process stands in sharp contrast with various recent attempts to create a "dialectical logic" which permits the occurrence of inconsistencies without thereby engendering any wholesale disaster from the logic at issue. It is in order to take a brief look at several projects along these lines.

Marxist dialectics

As Soviet theoreticians have developed it in recent times, in the wake of Engels' intimations, it is the characteristic feature of dialectical theory to espouse "the dogmatic assertion that there are real contradictions in the world"[1]—that in any given stage of world history contradictions can hold for certain theses and their negations will both be true together. In the wake of these ramifications of Marxist theory, various recent Soviet writers have endeavored to devise a "dialectical logic"—which is not, however, a "logic" in the sense of modern logical theory, but rather in the older, nineteenth-century, metaphysical mode that took its inspiration from Hegel.[2] The idea is

1. Nicholas Lobkowicz, *Das Wiederspruchsprinzip in der neueren Sowjetischen Philosophie* (Dordrecht, 1959) and "The Principle of Contradiction in Recent Soviet Philosophy," *Studies in Soviet Thought* 1 (1961):44–50.

2. The best general account of Soviet logic is Jürg Hänggi, *Formale und dialektische Logik in der Sowjetphilosophie* (Winterthur, 1971) and its bibliographic companion volume *Bib-*

to clothe the older framework of a Marx-Engels Hegelianism with trappings borrowed from various aspects of modern science. The utility and promise of such metaphysical theorizing is a matter of dispute—even in the Soviet Union itself. (In the West it has usually been dismissed out of hand.[3]) Recently, however, various formal logicians—particularly in eastern Europe—have tried to articulate these theories in the rigorous format of a formal calculus. This gives the matter a rather different aspect, to which we shall return below.

Formal reconstructions of the Hegelian dialectic

Over the past decade there have been various efforts to provide a "rational reconstruction" of the formal apparatus of Hegel's dialectic, using the mechanisms of symbolic logic.[4] This new venture in Hegel-interpretation may or may not eventually yield results which succeed on their proper ground of providing the basis for a new and better understanding of Hegel's philosophical ideas. However, quite independently of this, they have a substantial interest in their own right, as producing logical formalisms of novel types. Moreover, they also provide stimulus and support to the expanding project of developing formal logics of inconsistency to which we now turn.

liographie der Sowjetischen Logik (Winterthur, 1971). For other critical surveys of the relevant literature, see: I. M. Bochenski, "Soviet Logik," Studies in Soviet Thought 1 (1961): 29–38; T. J. Blakeley, Review article, Studies in Soviet Thought 3 (1963): 165–166; David Dinsmore Caney, "Current Trends in Soviet Logic," Inquiry 9 (1966): 94–108. Nicholas Lobkowicz, "The Principle of Contradiction in Recent Soviet Philosophy," Studies in Soviet Thought 1 (1961): 44–50; G. A. Wetter, Soviet Ideology Today (New York, 1966); J. M. Bochenski, The Dogmatic Principles of Soviet Philosophy (as of 1958) (Dordrecht, 1963); G. L. Kline's review article (of articles in Voprosy filosofii discussing the relationship of formal logic and dialectical logic), in the Journal of Symbolic Logic 18 (1958): 83–86; H. B. Acton, "Dialectical Materialism" in The Encyclopedia of Philosophy, ed. by Paul Edwards, Vol. 2 (New York, 1967), pp. 384–397.

3. For example, Alonzo Church unblushingly cites "the incompatibility of logic and dialectic" as a principal reason why "Soviet logic will not develop fruitfully or successfully." (Review of A. Philipov's Logic and Dialectic in the Soviet Union, Journal of Symbolic Logic 18 (1958): 272–273.)

4. See, for example, Michael Kosok, "The Formalization of Hegel's Dialectical Logic," International Philosophical Quarterly 6 (1966): 596–631; reprinted in A. MacIntyre (ed.), Hegel: A

"Dialectical" symbolic logics

Recent years have seen a diversified spate of attempts to construct formal systems of symbolic logic that are capable of admitting inconsistencies without vitiating consequences.[5] A forerunner here was a pioneering 1948 paper by the Polish logician Stanislaw Jaskowski,[6] but the main thrust of effort is more recent. A great deal of work has been done since the early 1960s by the Brazilian logician Newton C. A. Da Costa and his associates,[7] who have tried to devise suitable systems of inconsistency-tolerating "dialectical" logic, intending to provide for an inconsistent set theory in which Russell's paradox is derivable, but which nevertheless avoids hyperinconsistency. Other contributions in this general direction of dialectical logic include papers by F. G. Asenjo,[8] S. K. Thomason,[9] Richard and Valerie Routley,[10] Robert K. Meyer,[11] and others. (This literature is only now beginning to reach a stage of rapid growth—at this writing, much of it is accessible only in preprint versions.) The relevance logic of A. R. Anderson and N. D. Belnap, Jr. and their associates should also be mentioned under this head.[12]

Collection of Critical Essays (Garden City, 1972). See also Dominique Dubarle and André Doz, *Logique et dialectique* (Paris, 1972) and A. Sarlemijn, *Hegel's Dialectic* (Dordrecht, 1975) which offer helpful bibliographies.

5. A very useful survey is given in Robert G. Wolf, *Contradictions and Logical Systems* (unpublished).

6. Stanislaw Jaskowski, "Un calcul des propositions pour les systèmes deductifs contradictoires," *Studia Societatis Scientiarum Torunensis*, 1 (1948): 55–57. (Cf. note 3, Appendix 1.)

7. The starting point was da Costa's 1963 doctoral dissertation at the Federal University of Parana: *Sistemas formais inconsistentes*. A useful recent exposition of the work of da Costa's and his collaborators is given in his paper, "On the Theory of Inconsistent Formal Systems," *Notre Dame Journal of Formal Logic* 15 (1974): 497–510, which gives a full bibliography.

8. F. G. Asenjo, "A Calculus of Antinomies," *Notre Dame Journal of Formal Logic* 7 (1966): 103–105.

9. S. K. Thomason, "Towards a Formalization of Dialectical Logic," forthcoming. (See the abstract in the *Journal of Symbolic Logic* 39 [1974] 204.)

10. Richard and Valerie Routley, *Beyond the Actual* (forthcoming). Richard Routley and Robert K. Meyer, "Dialectical Logic, Classical Logic, and the Consistency of the World," *Dialectics and Humanism* (forthcoming).

11. Meyer's joint paper with Routley and Meyer see Richard and Valerie Routley, *Beyond the Actual*, which gives a forceful and cogent defense of the aims and prospects of dialectical logic.

12. See Alan R. Anderson and Nuel D. Belnap, Jr., *Entailment* (Princeton, 1975).

The Meinong revival

The 1970s have seen a rapid rise in the stock of Meinong's *Gegenstandstheorie* on the marketplace of philosophy.[13] In particular, several logicians have recently sought to rehabilitate Meinong's theory of "impossible" objects.[14] It is no exaggeration to say that a small but powerful "back to Meinong" movement is astir, a movement which lends yet another dimension of support to the demise of the traditional flight from inconsistency.

All of these lines of development represent attempts to implement a common leading idea—that of devising a body of theoretical machinery that will tolerate selfcontradictory theses within a framework of rational inquiry. In this regard they differ in orientation from our present approach, where actual selfcontradictions (in the rigid and classical logical sense of that term) are never permitted to arise.

13. The *fons et origo* of this enterprise is Alexius Meinong (1853–1920). See his essay "Ueber Gegenstandstheorie" (1904), reprinted in Vol. II of his *Gesammelte Abhandlungen*, 2 vols (Leipzig, 1713–4), and tr. in R. M. Chisholm (ed.), *Realism and the Background of Phenomenology* (Glencoe, Ill., 1960). And see also his *Ueber die Stellung der Gegenstandstheorie im System der Wissenschaften* (Leipzig, 1907).

14. The recent literature includes: Hector-Neri Castañeda, "Thinking and the Structure of the World," unpublished; Roderick M. Chisholm, "Beyond Being and Nonbeing," in Rudolf Haller (ed.), *Jenseits von Sein und Nichtsein: Beiträge zur Meinong-Forschung* (Graz, 1972), pp. 25–36; *idem*, "Homeless Objects," *Revue internationale de Philosophie* 104/5 (1973): 207–223; J. N. Findlay, *Meinong's Theory of Objects and Values*, 2nd ed. (Oxford, 1963); L. Goddard and R. Routley, *The Logic of Significance and Context*, vol. 1 (Aberdeen, 1973); Guido Küng, "Noema und Gegenstand," in Rudolf Haller (ed.), *Jenseits von Sein und Nichtsein: Beiträge zur Meinong-Forschung*, pp. 55–62; Karel Lambert, "Impossible Objects," *Inquiry* 17 (1974): pp. 303–314; *idem*, "On 'The Durability of Impossible Objects'," *Inquiry* 19 (1976): 251–253; *idem*, "Review Discussion: The Theory of Objects," *Inquiry* 16 (1973): 221–230; Terence Parsons, "A Prolegomenon to Meinongian Semantics," *The Journal of Philosophy* 71 (1974): 561–580; Richard Routley, "Exploring Meinong's Jungle: Items and Descriptions," *Notre Dame Journal of Formal Logic* 18 (1977), and *idem*, "The Durability of Impossible Objects," *Inquiry* 19 (1976): 247–251; Richard and Valerie Routley, "Rehabilitating Meinong's Theory of Objects," *Revue Internationale de Philosophie* 27 (1973): 224–254; S. K. Thomason, "Towards a Formulation of Dialectical Logic" (forthcoming).

Appendix 2
Dialogue as
an instrument
of logical
exposition

It is a perhaps justifiable digression also to mention the potential utility of dialectical devices as a method of demonstration in formal logic
itself. This approach is due originally to Paul Lorenzen and has been
developed by him and his collaborators, and especially by Kuno
Lorenz.[1] It envisages a dialogical strategy of proof development, with
demonstration proceeding as a sort of dialogical game, alternating between stages of challenge (attack) and substantiation (defense). These
moves are made in conformity with a schedule of formal rules of
argumentation (the analogue of the usual rules of inference). The
whole process is subject to the specification of a winning position (a
proof-termination rule). (The resultant dialogue-games for propositional logic bear a rough analogy with the more familiar proof tech-

1. The basic papers of Paul Lorenzen are: *Einführung in die operative Logik und Mathematik*
(Berlin/Göttingen/Heidelberg, 1955); *Formale Logik,* 3rd ed. (Berlin, 1967); "Logik und
Agon," *Atti del XII Congresso Internazionale di Filosofia: Venezia 1958* (Firenze, 1958), part 4
pp. 187–194; "Ein dialogisches Konstruktivitätskriterium" in Polish Academy of Sciences,
Infinitistic Methods: Proceedings of the Symposium on Foundations of Mathematics: Warsaw 1959
(Oxford, 1961); *Methodisches Denken* (Frankfurt a.M., 1968); *Normative Logik and Ethics*
(Mannheim, 1969); P. Lorenzen and W. Kamlah, *Logische Propädeulik,* 2nd ed. (Mannheim,
1967); and Paul Lorenzen and Oswald Schwemmer, *Konstructive Logik, Ethik und Wissenschaftstheorie* (Mannheim, 1974; 2nd ed., 1975). The relevant workings by Kuno Lorenz
include: *Arithmetik und Logik als Spiele* (Kiel, 1961); "Dialogispiele als semantische Grundlagen
von Logikkalkülen," *Archiv fur mathematische Logik und Grundlagenforschung* 11 (1968): 32–55
and 73–100; "Rules versus Theorems," *Journal of Philosophical Logic* 2 (1973): 352–369. See also
Wolfgang Stegmüller, "Remarks on the Completeness of Logical Systems Relative to the Validity Concepts of P. Lorenzen and K. Lorenz," *Notre Dame Journal of Formal Logic* 5 (1964):
81–112, and Horst Wessell, "Eine dialogische Begründung der logischen Gesetze" in *idem*
(ed.), *Quantoren-Modaletäten-Paradoxien* (Berlin, 1972), pp. 256–277.

nique based on the use of semantical tableaux.) As the dialogical game proceeds, the sequence of defensive responses to successive challenges-to-substantiate eventuates in the development of a formal proof within the logical system at issue. Disputation ends in demonstration.

This interesting device exhibits the usefulness of a disputational mechanism in an area of discussion—viz., formal logic—that is different from, but not unrelated to, the sphere of factual inquiry towards which the deliberations of the present book are oriented.

5 What justifies the dialectical rationale of probative rationality?

1. Acceptance and probative standards

The preceding discussion has contended that the probative ground rules governing the constructing of a persuasive case, a "good argument" for accepting factual contentions about the world, may with advantage be regarded as ultimately based on a dialectical paradigm. It was held that rationale-construction has *rational controversy* for its originating model and that it is subject to essentially the same standards. But *origination* does not determine *justification*, and so the question remains: are our argumentative ground rules actually effective towards this end? What is the basis of their legitimacy? The issue of the justification of the dialectical rationale of probative rationality thus comes to the fore, and it sets the prime task for the present chapter.

Men accept various contentions about the world they live in, and, being rational animals, they do so on the basis of grounds and reasons (be they good or bad). Now there are two dimensions of risk relating to such acceptance: the *practical* (suffering bad consequences; undergoing pain or frustration), and the *theoretical* (falling into error; being wrong). A fundamental interconnection obtains between these two risks of acceptance in the face of uncertainty in that there is a crucial trade-off between them in rational deliberation: if the practical risk of error is great, the theoretical should be small, and *vice versa,* where the practical risk of error is small, the theoretical may be allowed to be greater. This relationship between theoretical and practical risk represents a fundamental fact of the rational enterprise, and it is crucial in this regard that one be able to carry out a kind of intellectual or cognitive cost-benefit analysis for appraising theoretical risks. Any adequate epistemological theory accordingly requires a mechanism for appraising theoretical risk. And since the assessment of theoretical risk will have to proceed on the basis of determining the strength of the case that can be built up on behalf of the thesis in view, the probative issue of "building a good case" for a thesis becomes a central problem in the theory of knowledge.

This matter of "building a good case" for a thesis involves two things: (1) assessing the strength of the case for it when *taken by itself*, through determining the preponderance of pros over cons, and (2) assessing the strength of the case for it *on a comparative basis* with respect to its rivals, the other alternatives at hand. In furnishing the natural means for the realization of these objectives, the process of dialectic—of rational controversy—emerges as a crucial tool of cognitive rationality. The probative mechanisms which afford us an instrument for an epistemically or cognitively construed cost-benefit analysis—exhibiting, analyzing, and weighing the pros and cons of thesis-acceptance—thereby furnish a requisite of rationality, providing an instrument indispensable to its operation.

But, of course, the important thing is not just that such a process of probative cost-benefit analysis should take place, but that it should take place "correctly," that is, *rationally,* in an appropriate and defensible way. The issue of validating the mechanisms of probative rationality thus becomes a pressing one.

There is no rationality without an appropriate procedure for giving a *rationale*—a suitable fabric of good reasons in cases of the sort at issue. The analysis and evaluation of probative reasoning forms a crucial part of the theory of rationality. It is an essential aspect of the very nature of the rational enterprise to subscribe to a reasonable standard of probative procedure with respect to evidential relations, presumptions, plausibility, and the rest of it. Accordingly, one must explore the considerations which validate such standard items of probative practice as, for example, giving greater credence according to

76

factors of source reliability, supportive evidence, and inductive systematicity. It thus becomes necessary to examine the legitimating basis for our machinery of probative practice, and to ask: just what are the credentials of the established probative rules—the standard machinery of evidence, plausibility, presumption, etc.?

2. Probative mechanisms as requisites of rationality

The emphasis on rationality in probative practice leads back to the earlier distinction between "conventional" and "natural" dialectic. As we have seen, the rules of probative procedure in some contexts—law and disputation preeminently—can be designedly artificial (e.g., by disqualifying certain witnesses capable of providing materially relevant data or by conventionally setting up certain proof-texts as an unquestionable "gospel"). But the *natural* ground rules of probative rationality sweep all these artificialities aside. It is not a matter of abiding by artificial rules, but rather of doing what is "the right and proper thing" in the setting of rational argumentation.

Cognitive rationality has two significantly distinguishable aspects. Both *thesis-introduction moves* and *thesis-derivation moves* are indispensable to the dialectical enterprise of rational argumentation in discourse or discussion:

(1) *Formal or inferential rationality* in relation to the mutual bearing of beliefs in point of their consistency and their mutual implications. This has to do with the inner articulation of a person's belief-system (and hence is a *formal* issue of the internal makeup of the collection of theses that constitute that system). Here the key question is: does the person abide by the established inferential ground rules? This is primarily a matter of maintaining consistency among beliefs, of recognizing the consequences of accepted beliefs, and acknowledging the acceptability of the recognized consequences of accepted theses.

(2) *Substantive or evidential rationality* in relation to the *utilization of evidence*. This has to do with the initial introduction of accepted

77

theses into a person's belief-system (and hence is a *material* issue of the substantive content of that system). Here the key question is: does the person abide by the established *evidential* ground rules in coordinating his credence with the evidence in hand and with the ground rules of plausibility and presumption?

Cognitive rationality embraces *both* of these aspects of evidential thesis-introduction and inferential thesis-attunement within a coherently articulated belief-system. In particular, rational argumentation demands reason-presenting moves that reflect the probative ground rules revolving about the concepts of burden of proof. The ramifications of plausibility and presumption are accordingly pivotal in determining what it is to provide adequate epistemic basis for rational acceptance. The crucial linkage between presumption and rationality rests on the underlying thesis that a warranted presumption is one which should carry weight with the rational man, and that the rational man is prepared to accord to presumptions the weight that is their just due.

These considerations indicate the key role of such probative mechanisms for rational inquiry. Their status is determined by their functional task; they provide instruments basic to the working of rationality in probative contexts. To break the rules of proper argumentation is, in the final analysis, to opt out of the enterprise of rational controversy. It reflects a failure of rationality through a refusal to abide by the rules that define what it is to make out a proper case in the context of reasoned discussion.

But is such a break of the accustomed rules all that bad?

3. Is Rationality a Matter of Ethics?

Why should one endorse the standard ground rules of rationality and accept their probative concomitants? Indeed: *why be rational?* What is at issue here is not the epistemologists' usual question, "How ought one to conduct one's cognitive affairs rationally—how does one 'play the rationality game,' as it were?" but the even more basic issue posed by the sceptic's question: "Why should one 'play the rationality game' at all?"

Is this perhaps a matter of ethics and moral philosophy? For it may be, as C. I. Lewis has maintained, that "cognitive correctness is itself a moral concern, in the broad sense of 'moral'." [1]

When the rules of evidence are violated in argumentation or reasoning, a person "has no *right*" to be persuaded because "a *proper* case" has not been made out. What is the force here of *right* and *proper?* Do these normative and deontic terms here bear their familiar ethical or moral sense?

W. K. Clifford certainly thought so. In his classic 1877 essay on "The Ethics of Belief" (to which William James' even more famous essay of 1895 on "The Will to Believe" offered a reply) Clifford maintained his famous thesis that:

> It is wrong, always, everywhere and for anyone, to believe anything upon insufficient evidence. [2]

Some writers have even gone so far as to push this approach to its logical conclusion by pressing it towards the boundaries that separate the morally reprehensible from the legally criminal. For example, in

---

1. C. I. Lewis, *Values and Imperatives,* ed. by J. Lange (Stanford, 1969), p. 163. This work canvasses various issues relevant to the present discussion. (Its ultimate upshot does not differ greatly from that of the present discussion, since Lewis's broad sense of "morality" encompasses prudence.)

2. *Lectures and Essays* (London, 1879), Vol. II; originally published in the *Contemporary Review* 30 (1877): 42–54. For a useful outline of the James-Clifford controversy and its background, see Peter Kauber, "The Foundations of James' Ethics of Belief," *Ethics* 84 (1974): 151–166, where the relevant issues are set out and further references to the literature are given. For a particularly interesting recent treatment, see Roderick Chisholm, "Lewis' Ethics of Belief," in *The Philosophy of C. I. Lewis,* ed. by P. A. Schilpp (La Salle, 1968), pp. 223 ff. In actual fact Clifford did not adhere to this hyperbolic standard throughout his epistemology. Rejecting the prospect of certainty in the area of scientific knowledge, he took the line that man's scientific "knowledge" of nature rests on various principles that are not in the final analysis justified on cognitive grounds at all, but must be accounted for in terms of natural selection. The principle of the uniformity of nature is a prime example, and "Nature is selecting for survival those individuals and races who act as if she were uniform; and hence the gradual spread of that belief over the civilized world." (*The Common Sense of the Exact Sciences* [London, 1885], p. 209.) Clifford is thus constrained to resort to a rather otiose distinction between (as it were) "ideally secure" and "effectively well-grounded" beliefs, a distinction whose futility is marked by the fact that our factual "knowledge" is—whenever genuinely general—inevitably bound to fall into the second category.

Janet Chance's ardent little book on *Intellectual Crime,* one finds "the making of statements that outstrip the evidence" prominently enrolled on the register of this category of "crimes." [3]

William James quite properly argued against Clifford that the enterprise of inquiry is governed not only by the negative injunction "avoid error!" but no less importantly by the positive injunction "achieve truth!". And, in the factual area—where the *content* of our claims outstrips the evidence we can ever gather for them—this (so he insists) demands the risk of error. There is nothing irrational about accepting this risk, quite to the contrary: "a rule of thinking which would absolutely prevent one from acknowledging certain kinds of truth, if those kinds of truth were really there, would be an irrational rule." [4] Agreeing with James as to the irrationality involved, we maintain that no specifically *ethical* or *moral* obligation is operative in the injunctions. The issue is one of self-deprivation rather than one of moral turpitude. The obligation to be rational is not a *moral* obligation, and lapses from rationality are not *moral* lapses.

In the light of our present analysis, Clifford's ethicomoral interpretation must be rejected. The relevantly operative concept is that of the proper management of rational discussion, argumentation, and exposition. The fundamental issue is not one of *morality* but one of *rationality*—of intellectual rather than ethical standards. The rules of ethics and morality are correlative with the purpose of avoiding damage to the rights and interests of people—preeminently *other* people. By contrast, the person who violates the evidential rules simply manages to reason badly. The probative rules are correlative with certain specific purposes, primarily the acquisition of truth. The interests that the man who departs from these rules damages are in the first instance his own—in falling away from the principles of right reason into irrationality, he frustrates his own aims and objectives (with certainty his *cognitive* objectives and with probability his *practical* objectives). The resultant sanctions fall directly and immediately upon him himself, and upon others (if at all) more or less accidentally.

The person who is defective in point of rationality—who reasons inadequately, thinks poorly, and argues badly—is akin to the person

3. Janet Chance, *Intellectual Crime* (London, 1933), pp. 33–34.
4. *The Will to Believe and Other Essays in Popular Philosophy* (New York, 1956), pp. 27–28.

who is defective in point of intelligence, and his offenses are not *sins* but *gaffes*. Both are more to be pitied than censured. (Of course, the case of *deliberate* transgression is a very different one. Insofar as reckless assertion beyond the available evidence may, when given credence, cause others to have and act on mistaken beliefs, it can also, of course, be a matter of wrong-doing—certainly so when this results from faults of character [e.g., cupidity] rather than faults of intellect [e.g., stupidity]. Undoubtedly, the person who sets out *deliberately to deceive others* by means of improper reasoning is morally culpable, just as the person who sets out to offend others deliberately by boorish behavior. But that's altogether another matter.)

In the ethical case *"ought"* demands *"can."* But *can* we avoid accepting factual claims on less than guaranteeing evidence: do we really have an option here? Clearly not, once we make the prime commitment to rationality and insist on the appropriate guidance of action by belief. For this demands that we do make fact-involving commitments. And if the *content* of factual claims by their very nature outstrips the reach of the evidence (and not just the evidence we *do* have but the evidence we *can* have), then we cannot justly be reproached for accepting theses upon "insufficient" evidence. The rational guidance of praxis demands evidence-transcending commitments.[5] Just this is the burden of James' case against Clifford.[6]

Consider the following further objection:

> Even if you are right in holding that what is at issue is a matter of the procedural principles of rationality, does this not still generate an ethical aspect through the higher-level principle that *People ought to be rational?*

Of course, people *ought* to be rational—this is something that one must admit and indeed insist upon. But this "ought" is surely not a *moral* ought. For people ought also to be perceptive, sensitive, in-

---

5. "Someone who says 'Better go without belief forever than believe a lie!' merely shows his own preponderant private horror of becoming a dupe . . . but I can believe that worse things than being duped may happen to a man in this world. . . ." William James, *The Will to Believe and Other Essays in Popular Philosophy* (New York, 1956), pp. 16–17.

6. For an interesting analysis of the James-Clifford controversy, see Alex C. Michalos, "The Morality of Cognitive Decision-Making," in M. Brand and D. Walton (eds.), *Action Theory* (Dordrecht, 1976).

telligent, open-minded, etc. The "ought" here is not, however, an *ethical* ought, but one of the cosmic fitness of things. It does not indicate an operative principle of human action, but represents an idealized vision of the optimal arrangements of the world.[7] The world *ought* to be a place where things go properly. But people have no more a *duty* to be good believers than they have a *duty* to be good rememberers, however desirable it may be in the larger scheme of things for them to be so.[8] No moral obligation is at issue. The crucial point is that the rules of evidence are principles of rational argumentation which define what is "right and proper" in a *procedural* sense relating to the adequate conduct of inquiry, and this is something quite different from the "right and proper" of ethical evaluation or moral criticism.

But if no *moral* obligation is at issue in cognitive rationality, then just what's wrong with being cognitively agnostic? Why not simply "play safe," let caution be the better part of (epistemic) valor and systematically refrain from accepting anything? Particularly if (or rather, *since*) our knowledge of objective fact is always defeasible—in that our cognitive claims about the objective circumstances of the world here are in general *potentially* flawed—abstention might well be the best policy.[9] Indeed, why not adopt the sceptic's traditional stance of an all-out suspension of judgment, thereby saving ourselves the trouble of having any probative ground rules at all? This crucial question sets the stage for the next two chapters.

7. Of course, whenever such an "ought" of cosmic fitness is operative, there is a correlative duty to cultivate and promote its realization. But this represents quite a different issue. People ought to speak correctly or do thier sums properly. But that does not make departures from correct speech or correct arithmetic *ethical* transgressions.

8. The "ought" at issue is what I have elsewhere called that of *evaluative metaphysics* in contrast with that of *normative ethics*. ("The Dimensions of Metaphysics," in *Essays in Philosophical Analysis* [Pittsburgh, 1969], pp. 229–254.) The relationship between these two modes of deontology is explored in that essay.

9. Thus compare Carnap's agnostically acceptance-phobic stance towards those factual propositions that involve any element of generality. Cf. Rudolf Carnap, *Logical Foundations of Probability* (Chicago, 1950).

6 A dialectically based critique of scepticism

1. Cognitive scepticism

The preceding chapter has considered the nature of probative rationality in the cognitive domain. It is appropriate in its sequel to discuss the principal aberration of this rationality, namely scepticism.

Unlike its specifically *religious* counterpart, the historic doctrine of *cognitive* scepticism is agnostic specifically with regard to man's capacity to attain knowledge about the world of nature and its contents and doings. The appropriate antonym here would be *cognitivism*—a doctrine holding that well-warranted claims to knowledge can indeed be made in this factual sphere.[1]

The cognitive sceptic does not hold that what we think we know about the world is *false*. He simply maintains that our knowledge-claims in this domain are unwarranted—that we inevitably lack due justification for making them. He regards the evidential basis we normally invoke in support of such knowledge-claims as inevitably being probatively insufficient. The sceptic exploits the fact that the unending why/because cycle of question and answer can also be traversed with respect to claim and grounding:

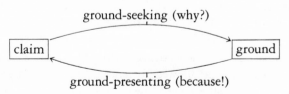

ground-seeking (why?)

claim   ground

ground-presenting (because!)

1. For the classical doctrines, see Charlotte L. Stough, *Greek Scepticism* (Berkeley and Los Angeles, 1969). A good contemporary statement of the position is Peter Unger, *Ignorance: A*

The sceptic revels in the endless regress inherent in such a cycle. He insists that we can never know anything because knowledge must be altogether certain—secure against every question—whereas the list of potential questions is always endless.

2. Scepticism and rationality

A useful way of viewing scepticism is to regard it from the perspective of the standard probative ground rules—particularly the ideas of presumption and burden of proof. From this angle it appears that the sceptic simply *rejects* the usual common-sense practice of granting a presumption of veracity to our senses, our memory, our practices of inductive reasoning, and the like, thus denying the serviceability of the very materials from which alone our knowledge of the world is—or can be—constructed. Accordingly, the sceptic moves towards such positions as agnosticism regarding factual matters, personalistic solipsism in abstaining from belief in the existence of other people, cognitive solipsism in the rejection of the vicarious evidence of others, etc. All these positions are immediate consequences of rejecting the presumptive veracity of such cognitive resources as the senses, memory, inductive inference, and the like.

The ordinary and standard probative practice of empirical inquiry stipulates a presumption in favor of the senses, of memory, the inductive ground rules, etc. We accept the claims derived from these sources as veridical until proven otherwise. When the sceptic refuses to grant this presumption, he effectively blocks any prospect of reasoning with him within the standard framework of discussion about the empirical facts of the world.

Throughout the sphere of empirical reason, the rules of probative praxis must be allowed to do their proper work of showing where presumptions lie and how the burden of argumentation can be shifted—one cannot be allowed to redesign them so as to cut one's opposition off from all further prospect of argumentation. The victory won by the man who systematically refuses to grant the evidential

Case for Scepticism (Oxford, 1975). See also Keith Lehrer, "Why Not Scepticism?", *The Philosophical Forum* 2 (1971): 283–298.

84

weight of considerations contrary to his position is at once inevitable and empty. Scepticism profoundly misreads the dialectical situation: it insists on taking the *initial* situation (viz., a burden of proof against the thesis maintained at the outset) as *ultimate* (viz., a burden of proof against *every* contention, even those introduced supportively at later stages).

When it comes to the validation of our empirical beliefs about the contingent arrangement of what goes on in the world, the sceptic in effect refuses to adopt the usual probative/evidential rules of procedure. When we adduce the data of the senses, of memory, etc., in support of such beliefs, the sceptic simply denies their probative weight. "You admit," he says in a Cartesian tone of voice, "that these data sources occasionally deceive you; so how can you be confident that they do not go amiss in the case in hand?" Given that the only sort of evidence we could possibly adduce in the specific circumstances will itself have to be of the very type whose probative weight the sceptic calls into question, we have no way of meeting his argument head-on. But surely, whatever victory the Pyrrhonian sceptic is able to gain by this sort of strategy will have to be altogether Pyrrhic.

One need not read long in the sceptical literature to see just how the sceptic runs afoul of burden-of-proof considerations. Take perception-based claims. "That is a window" will do for an example. The sceptic immediately protests: "How can you be certain?" And he proceeds to deploy the whole Cartesian demonology with which we are all too familiar. How can we be so sure a deceitful spirit is not at work with lights and mirrors? How can we guarantee the whole of our cognitive life is not being staged for a pickled brain by a mad scientist playing a tape? How can we tell that the totality of our perceptions is not being arranged on another planet by clever beings affecting our brains with electrostatic discharges? In sum: what categorical assurances can be obtained that the whole stage of our experience is not merely one vast Potemkin village?

Burden-of-proof considerations sweep all such worries aside. They say in effect: "Do not plague me with these merely hypothetical possibilities. If there are any positive, *case-specific,* indications that here and now, in the concrete circumstances of this particular claim, mirrors may be involved or evil scientists at work, well and good. Let us look into the matter more closely. But purely conjectural hypothetical possibilities just don't count in probative situations. What does count is only what the available evidence indicates to be a genuine prospect under the circumstances."

But even accepting the previous argument of a need for standards of plausibility and presumption, a sceptical objector may press the issue yet further, arguing as follows:

> The preceding line of reasoning shows the need to admit—in interests of rationality—SOME canons (standards, principles) of presumption and proof. But why should one accept *these* (our actual) probative standards? *Quis custodiet ipsos custodies?* Upon what validating considerations do the probative standards of presumption and proof themselves rest?

And this line is not without its merits. There will, to be sure, have to be some appropriate rationale of justification for our probative ground rules. And if it were simply this legitimation that the sceptic is asking for, his demands would not be unreasonable and could always in principle be met. But in transmuting the need to justify the principles for allocating benefit of doubt into a ground for distorting the nature of this allocation—turning it, in effect, against the theses it initially favored—the sceptic takes an unwarranted step that vitiates his position.

After all, if it were simply a *request for justification* that were at issue, then this would have to be understood as itself subject to the appropriate ground rules of evidence in the building up of a justificatory case. But in undertaking a blanket rejection of the usual principles of presumption and benefit of doubt, the sceptic renders it in principle impossible to provide the sort of case he demands. Accordingly, the sceptic's stance, in effect, begs the question (perhaps "begs the conclusion" would be better) by laying down conditions which block from the very outset the development of the case he challenges his opponent to produce.

On his home ground of purely theoretical argumentation regarding abstract possibilities, the sceptic's position is no doubt secure and irrefutable. By refusing to accept the standard probative grounds *as grounds*—as capable of constituting a rational basis of warrant for acceptance—the sceptic assures the security of his position. He thus wins an easy—but empty—victory because he sets up a standard for "knowledge" so hyperbolic that he *systematically denies evidential weight to those considerations which alone could be brought to bear in making out a case to the contrary.* This very fact marks the profound unreasonableness of the sceptic's position. Skepticism inclines to the hypertrophy of a cognitive standard: one of the usual criteria of knowledge has become exaggerated and inflated beyond any feasible prospect of satisfaction.

In cases where the evidential indications are strong enough, the burden of rationality shifts against the side of sceptical disbelief, precisely because the range of rational warrant inevitably outstrips that of demonstrative proof. To say "I know" or "He knows" is to claim or concede knowledge. Here, as with any other factual thesis that stakes a claim which—at least in principle—goes partially beyond the evidence, the claim that is staked may have to be withdrawn. To assert this claim in the strong language of "knowledge" is indeed to say that it is "inconceivable" that the claim would have to be withdrawn. But this inconceivability is not of a *theoretical* but of a *practical* nature. The cognitivist holds that a perfectly justified knowledge-claim may in the event prove wrong, but yet that—recognizing and conceding this—one may be entirely justified in insisting that *in this case* such a theoretical prospect can reasonably be put aside.

Philosophical sceptics generally set up some abstract standard of absolutistic certainty and then proceed to show that no knowledge-claims in a certain area (sense, memory, scientific theory, etc.) can possibly meet the conditions of this standard. From this fact the impossibility of such a category of "knowledge" is accordingly inferred. But this inference is totally misguided. For surely what actually follows is simply the inappropriateness or incorrectness of the standard at issue. If the vaunted standard is such that knowledge-claims cannot possibly meet it, the appropriate moral is not "too bad for knowledge-claims," but rather "too bad for the standard." The sceptic's argument is a double-edged sword that inflicts the more serious damage upon itself. It is senseless to impose on something conditions which it cannot in the very nature of things meet: the old Roman legal precept applies—*ultra posse nemo obligatur.* Once all that is reasonably possible—i.e., all that can *appropriately* be expected—has been done to assure some knowledge claim, it is unreasonable, nay irrational, to ask for more. The case for a knowledge-claim should indeed be "conclusive," but *conclusive* not in some absolutistic and in principle unrealizable sense, but in the sense of being as good a case as one can reasonably be asked to make out under the circumstances, considering the sort of thing at issue.

3. The role of certainty

But surely something's *being* certain—or even *being* true—in fact just is not a necessary precondition for *a rationally warranted claim* to knowledge. Consider the two propositions:

> *P* is justifiably held by *X* to be true.
> *P* is true.

Does the first entail or require the second? Surely not. For the evidence-in-hand that suffices to justify someone in holding a thesis to be true need not provide a *deductive* guarantee of this thesis. For a strictly analogous situation obtains with the pair:

> *P* is justifiably held by *X* to be certain.
> *P* is certain.

Again, the first proposition does not entail or require the second. The standard gap between the epistemic issue of what someone justifiably holds to be and the ontological issue of what *is* again comes into the picture. One must be willing to admit in general the existence of a gap between *warranted assertability* and ultimate *correctness,* holding that on occasion even incorrect theses can be maintained with due warrant. And there is no decisive reason for blocking the application of this general rule to knowledge-claims in particular.

Factual claims are invariably such that there is a wide gap between the *evidence* we need to have at our disposal to make a claim warrantedly and the *content* of this claim. The milkman leaves the familiar sort of bottle of white liquid on the doorstep. One does not hesitate to call it "milk." A small cylinder of hard, white, earthen material is lying next to the blackboard. One does not hesitate to call it "chalk." The *content* of such claims clearly ranges far wider than our meager ev-

88

idence and extends to chemical composition, sources of origin, behavior under pressure, etc., etc. And this story is a standard one. For the fact is that all of our statements regarding matters of objective fact (i.e., "That *is* an apple" as opposed to "Something appears to me to be an apple") are such that the *content* of the claim—its overall set of commitments and implications—moves far beyond the (relatively meager) evidence for it that is actually at our disposal.

Yet the rules of reasoned discourse are such that we are rationally entitled to make our descriptive claims—*notwithstanding* the literally endless implicative ramifications of their content, ramifications over whose obtaining we in fact have no rational control without making specific verificatory checks. And note that even if such checks were made, their results would be incomplete and would pertain to a few specific samples drawn from an infinite range.

And this state of things has an important application when knowledge-discourse is at issue. For here too we must distinguish between evidence and claim, between the *warrant* for a claim and its *content*.

The assertion "I *know* that *P*" has all of those absolutistic facets we have considered (certainty, unqualifiedness, etc.). All are ineliminably parts of the *content* of the claim. But with this particular factual claim, as with any other, one need not establish full rational control over the whole gamut of its entailments and implications. One can appropriately assert "I know that *P*" when one has adequate rational warrant for this assertion, and this warrant may well stop at *adequately conclusive*[2]—rather than *comprehensively exhaustive*—evidence for the claim.

The ground rules of rational discourse are such that when factual claims are at issue the thesis:

(1) I am rationally warranted to assert *P*

does *not* entail (or presuppose or otherwise require) the thesis

(2) I have rational control (of a certificatory or confirmatory character) over each and every constituent part of the commitment-content of *P*.

2. For example, we need not—in the usual course of things—be in a position to rule out the imaginative sceptic's recourse to uncannily real dreams, deceitful demons, etc.

The sphere of rational discourse regarding factual issues is such that there is a standard, inevitable, and perfectly acceptable *evidential gap* between the commitment content of our claims and the requisite *warranting evidence* at our disposal for making them (appropriately and justifiably). This circumstance is implicit in the very ground rules of rational discourse. To reject or impugn it is to cast aside the practice of verbal communication as we actually carry it on.

The thesis that knowledge must be *certain* requires critical scrutiny and analysis in the light of these considerations. For "certainty" here must *not* be construed to mean "derived by infallible processes from theoretically unassailable premisses" since one is surely justified in "being certain" in circumstances that do not *logically* preclude any possibility of error. The operative mode of "certainty" here is not some absolutistic sense of logical infallibility—it is the realistic concept that underlies our actual, real-life processes of argumentation and reasoning. It is impossible to give too heavy emphasis to the crucial fact that to say of a thesis that it "is certain" is to say no more than *it is as certain as, in the nature of the case, a thesis of this sort reasonably could be rendered.* And this does not—and need not—preclude *any* possibility of error, but any *real* or *genuine* possibility of error.

The cognitivist who claims in the sceptic's despite to know that P need not insist that he has intrinsically irrefutable and logically conclusive evidence that P. It is simply not necessary for him to make an assertion of this sort in support of his contention. It is sufficient that his evidence for P is as good as that for anything of P's type possibly would be. To be sure we must be certain of what we know, but the "certainty" that must attach to knowledge-claims need not be absolutistic in some way that is in principle unrealizable. It must be construed in the sense of *as certain as can reasonably be expected in the circumstance.* A claim to knowledge does not—as the sceptics charge—transgress by offering in principle infeasible guarantees; it simply means that one is to rest secure in the assurance that everything has indeed been done that one can possibly ask for within the limits of reasonableness to ascertain the fact at issue.

A rigidly parallel analysis must be made of the thesis that knowledge precludes any possibility of mistake. It is not any "logical" or "merely theoretical" prospect of mistake that is excluded, but any *real* possibility of being mistaken. This distinction between *absolute* and *real* possibilities of error is reflected in a parallel distinction between what might be termed *categorical* certainty on the one hand and *practical* or *effective* certainty on the other. The operative idea here is that of taking "every *proper* safeguard," or of doing "everything that can *reasonably* be asked" to assure the claim at issue. The evidential basis for effective certainty need not be "all the evidence there conceivably might be," but simply "all the evidence that might reasonably be asked for." It envisages that a stage could be reached when, even though further evidence might possibly be accumulated, there are no counterindications to suggest that this theoretically feasible prospect is practically desirable: there is *no reason* to think that further accumulation might be fruitful and *no reason* to believe that additional evidence might alter the situation.[3] And by "reason" here we must understand not some synoptic, wholesale, across-the-board consideration of the sort favored by sceptics since antiquity, but case-specific considerations that bear in a definite and *ad hoc* way upon the particular case in hand.

A claim to knowledge extends an assurance that all due care and caution has been exercised to ensure that any *real* possibility of error can be written off: it issues a guarantee that every proper safeguard has been exercised. Exactly this is the reason why the statement "I know *P*, but might be mistaken" is self-inconsistent. For the man who claims to know that *P* thereby issues a guarantee which the qualification "but I might be mistaken" effectively revokes. What is established by the self-defeating nature of locutions of the type of "I know that *P* but *might* well be wrong" is thus *not* that knowledge is inherently indefeasible, but simply that knowledge-claims offer guarantees and assurances so strong as to preempt any safeguarding qualifications: they preclude abridgment of the sort at issue in protective clauses like "I might well be wrong."

---

3. This "absence of counterindications" within the available evidence was indicated by the ancient Academic Sceptics in terms of the "concurrence" (*syndromē*) of evidence.

4. Scepticism and the rules of language

The sceptic sets up standards upon "knowledge" that are so unrealistic as to move outside the range of considerations at work in the conception as it actually functions in the language. He insists upon construing knowledge in such a way as to foist upon the cognitivist a Sisyphus-like task by subjecting all knowledge-claims to an effectively undischargeable burden of proof. But this hyperbolic standard separates the sceptic from the concept of knowledge as it functions in common life and in (most) philosophical discussions.

To be sure, the sceptic might well ask: "What gives you the right to impose *your* probative standards on *me?* How can you establish their propriety?" The answer is straightforward. If it is *knowledge* as the language deals with it that we wish to discuss—and not some artificial construct whose consideration constitutes a change of subject—then we must abide by the ground rules of the conceptual scheme that is at issue. And this simply is not a negotiable matter of playing the game by X's rules instead of Y's. It is not a conventional game that is defined by the rules we arbitrarily adopt, but an impersonal set of rules established in the public instrumentality of a language. We must not afford the sceptic the luxury of a permission to rewrite at his own whim the warranting standards for the terminology of our cognitive discourse.

The sceptic simply is not free to impose his hyperbolic probative standards upon us. If he wishes to dispute about *knowledge,* he must take the concept as he finds it in the language-based conceptual system that we actually use. (He cannot substitute a more rigoristic standard for *counting as knowledge,* any more than he can substitute a more rigoristic standard for counting as a dog, say a standard that ruled chihuahuas out as just too small.) In failing to make effective contact with the conceptual scheme in which our actual knowledge-claims in fact function, the sceptic assumes an irrational posture in the debate. And the crucial fact is that our actual standards here root in the ground rules for rational controversy and the conditions for making out a conclusive (probatively solid) case, ground rules and conditions in which all of the standard mechanisms of presumptions and burden of proof are embedded.

92

As Ayer has stressed, knowledge-claims are crucially predicated upon a "right to be sure."[4] But what is the nature of this right, and the *basis* of the warrant or entitlement at issue? The answer is simple: the *rules of language use* themselves. For a "language" involves not merely rules of meaning and rules of truth (semantical rules) and rules of inferential transition (logical rules) but rules of assertion-entitlement (evidential rules) as well. These last are warranting *rules* specifying the circumstances under which certain claims are in order—including what sorts of further circumstances abrogate such entitlements. The mastery of such ground rules is a crucial part of a child's language-learning. Language has an ineradicable "inductive" component—a built-in view of "the way in which things work in the world."[5]

Meaning rules and inference rules are familiar from logical and semantical discussions. But the no less important *warranting rules* that underlie our standard practice in verbal communication are comparatively unfamiliar. They may be relatively more variegated and less easy to codify. These are the ground rules of plausibility and presumption that indicate the standard bases on which claims stand "in the absence of counterindications" and that inventory the types of moves that defeat such claims. These rules specify, in effect, "how far is far enough" when it comes to closing the "evidential gap" in putting forward a (now duly warranted) assertion. These warranting rules are intrinsic components of the language—a part of what every child learns about his native tongue "at mother's knee."

5. Scepticism and praxis

The *traditional* pragmatic argument against sceptical agnosticism goes roughly as follows:

---

4. A. J. Ayer, *The Problem of Knowledge* (London, 1956), p. 35.
5. Compare Chapter Six of the author's *The Primacy of Practice* (Oxford, 1973). And see also John Pollock, *Knowledge and Justification* (Princeton, 1974), where it is argued that "The justification conditions of a statement are themselves constitutive of the meaning of the statement" (p. 21).

On the plane of abstract, theoretical reasoning the sceptical position is, to be sure, secure and irrefutable. But scepticism founders on the structure of the human condition—that man finds himself emplaced *in medias res* within a world where his very survival demands action. And the action of a rational being requires the guidance of belief. Not the inferences of theory and cognition but the demands of practice and action make manifest the untenability of the sceptic's position.

Conceding that scepticism cannot be defeated on its own ground, that of pure theory, it is held to be invalidated on *practical* grounds by an incapacity to support the requisites of human action. Essentially this argument is advanced by such diverse thinkers as the Academic Sceptics of classical antiquity, David Hume and William James.[6]

Unfortunately however, this position leaves it open for the sceptic to take to the high ground of a partisan of rigorous rationality. For the sceptic may well take the following line:

> This charge of stultifying practice is really beneath my notice. Theoretical reason and abstract rationality are what concerns the true philosopher. The issue of what is *merely practical* does not concern me. As far as "mere practice" goes, I am perfectly prepared to conform my actions to the pattern that men in general see fit to follow. But one should recognize that the demands of theoretical rigor point in another—and altogether sceptical—direction.[7]

The present line of argument does not afford the sceptic this comfortable option. Its fulcrum is not the issue of *practice* as such, but the issue of *rationality,* since it is our specifically *cognitive* practice of rational inquiry and argumentation that is at issue. In affecting to disdain *this* the sceptic must now turn his back not simply on the practice of ordinary life, but rationality itself. His "victory" is futile because he conveniently ignores the fact that the whole enterprise of reason-giving is aimed at *rationale construction* and is thus pointless save in the presence of a route to adequacy in this regard—the standard machinery for assessing probative propriety. The sceptic in effect emerges as unwilling to abide by the evidential ground rules that

6. In its fully developed form the argument goes back to the Academic Sceptic Carneades (c. 213-c. 128 B.C.) who headed the Platonic Academy; but its essentials are present in Pyrrho (c. 360-c. 270 B.C.), founder of the Sceptical school.

7. The sceptic might also hold that factual *knowledge* is not needed for praxis, since—so he could argue—mere *probability* suffices as a "guide to life."

govern the management of rational deliberation along the established lines.

In the final analysis, the sceptic thus runs afoul of the demands of that very rationality in whose name he so high-mindedly claims to speak. Rationality, after all, is not a matter of *logic* alone—of commitment to the logical principles of consistency (i.e., not to accept what contradicts accepted premises) and completeness (i.e., to accept what is entailed by accepted premises), which are, after all, purely hypothetical in nature ("If you accept . . . , then—"). For cognitive rationality turns—as we have seen—not upon probative derivation-moves alone but upon probative introduction-moves as well. It is not just a *hypothetical* issue of making proper inferences from given premisses; it involves also the *categorical* issue of giving their proper evidential weight to the premises themselves. Thus rationality indispensably requires a categorical and material constraint inherent in the conception of evidence—namely, to abide by the established evidential ground rules of various domains of discussion in terms of the locus of presumption and the allocation of benefit of doubt.

The sceptic is not embarked on a *defense* of reason, but on a self-imposed *exile* from the enterprise of rational discussion and the community of rational inquirers. And at this juncture he is no longer left in possession of the high ground. In refusing to give to the standard evidential considerations the presumptive and *prima facie* weight that is their established value on the market of rational interchange, the sceptic, rather than being the defender of rigid reason, is in fact profoundly irrational. The sceptic *seemingly* moves within the orbit of rationality. But by his refusal to acknowledge the ordinary probative rules of plausibility, presumption, evidence, etc., he effectively opts out of the rational enterprise in the interests of a private, idiosyncratic rigorism that results from attachment to an inappropriately hyperbolic standard.

6. Scepticism and the methodological turn

We have arrived at the contention that the sceptic is being unreasonable in that—by rejecting the established probative ground rules—he effectively withdraws from the arena of rationality, rejecting the basic rationale of reasonableness in the factual area at issue. But in striving against this conclusion, it remains open to the sceptic to argue as follows: "If I am departing from what on *your* view is 'rationality,' that doesn't show anything I'm prepared to regard as a genuine flaw. Indeed my very thesis is that your 'rationality' is, in a basic regard, deficient." To meet this desperate, but profound, objection we must shift the ground. It now becomes advantageous to stop talking about *beliefs* directly (the acceptance of *theses*) and to approach the whole issue from a new point of departure, namely, that of the rationality of practices, procedures, and methods.

In one of its classical forms, the sceptic's argument goes as follows:

> The rational man must, of course, have a basis for his beliefs and opinions. Thus, asked *why* he accepts some accepted belief or opinion, he will cite one (or more) others that support it. But we can now ask him why he accepts these in turn, and this process can be continued as long as one likes. As a result, we will either move in a circle—and so ultimately provide no justification at all—or become involved in an infinite regress, supporting the elephant on the back of a turtle on the back of an alligator, etc. The only way to terminate the regress is by a dogmatic acceptance, somewhere along the line, of an *ultimate* belief that is used to justify others but is not itself justified. But any such unjustified acceptance is by its very nature arbitrary and irrational.

But this position, while indeed strong, is not altogether unanswerable. The answer lies in recognizing that the things one rationally accepts are not of a piece. Specifically, it is necessary to give a careful heed to the essentially Kantian distinction between substantive *theses* on the one hand and regulative *methods* on the other.

It is indeed ultimately unsatisfactory to adopt the purely discursive course of justifying theses in terms of further theses and so on. But reflection on the structure of rational legitimation shows that this is not our only option. Rather, we justify our acceptance of certain factual theses because (ultimately) they are validated by the employment of a certain method, the scientific method. We thus break outside the cycle of justifying thesis by thesis, thanks to the fact that a thesis can be justified by application of a cognitive method. And then we justify the adoption of this method in its turn in terms of certain *practical*

96

criteria: success in prediction and efficacy in control. (With respect to *methodology*, at any rate, the pragmatists were surely in the right—there is certainly no better way of justifying a *method*—any method—than by establishing that "it works" with respect to the specific tasks held in view.)

This dialectic of justification thus breaks out of the restrictive confines of the sceptic's circle (or regress) and does so without relapse into a dogmatism of unjustified ultimates. We justify the acceptance of a thesis by reference to the method by which it is validated, justifying this method itself in terms of the classical pragmatic criterion of methodological validation.

This line of approach blocks the route towards philosophical scepticism by a complex, two-stage maneuver, combining the methodological justification of the *theses* that embody our claims to knowledge with the pragmatic justification of the cognitive *methods* by whose means these claims are certified. For now the sceptic cannot simply reject our orthodox "rationality" as misguided or deficient. The orientation towards cognitive methods—and so, correlatively, towards those basic aims and objectives at whose attainment these methods are oriented—averts any sceptical dismissal as supposedly unwarranted or irrelevant of the rationality at issue in their efficient realization. The sceptic cannot simply abandon our orthodox rationality without at the same time abandoning the cognitive and practical purposes it seeks to implement.

7. The pragmatic basis of cognition

The sceptic too readily looses sight of a crucial fact regarding the very *raison d'être* of our cognitive endeavors. Their aim—as we have seen—is not just to avoid error but to engross truth. The task of rational inquiry is to provide *information* about the world. And here, as elsewhere, "Nothing ventured, nothing gained" is the operative principle. To be sure, a systematic abstention from cognitive involvement is a sure-fire safeguard against error. But it affords this security at too steep a price, for it requires that one simply opt out of the cognitive enterprise.

97

Note that *this* line of thought does not involve any immediate resort to pragmatic considerations. Since the days of the Academic Sceptics of Greek antiquity, philosophers have often answered our present question "Why accept anything at all?" by taking roughly the following line: Man is a rational animal. *Qua* animal he must act—his very survival depends upon action. But *qua* rational being he cannot act availingly save insofar as his actions are guided by what he accepts. The *practical* circumstances of the human condition preclude the systematic suspension of belief as a viable policy.

But *this* sort of pragmatic appeal has not been operative in our present argumentation. Rather, our argument has addressed itself wholly to the issue of *cognitive* rationality. The line we take runs *not* "If one wants to act effectively then one one must accept certain theses," but rather "If one wants to enter into 'the cognitive enterprise'—that is, if one wants to be in the position to obtain information about the world—then one must be prepared to accept various theses." Both approaches take a line that is not categorical but rather hypothetical and conditional. But in the pragmatic case, the condition relates to the requisites for effective action, while in the cognitive case, it relates to the requisites for rational inquiry.

One could—to be sure—press the issue still one step further. For one might take the following line:

> Very well—let it be granted that acceptance is necessary to the project of rational inquiry or what you have called the "cognitive enterprise." So what? Why should one seek to play this "rationality game" at all? After all, to call someone "a rational person" is just giving him an honorific pat on the back for comporting himself in intellectual affairs in an approved manner. It begs—or leaves open—the questions: Why is this "rationality" really a good thing? What *point* is there to being rational?

We come here to the sceptic's case against the utility of reason. In war, victory does not always lie on the side of the big battalions. In inquiry, truth does not always lie on the side of the stronger reasons. And here we face the sceptic's final challenge: What basis is there for the belief that the real is rational (to put it in Hegelian terms)? What assurance do we have that aligning our beliefs with the canons of the logical and the reasonable leads us any closer to *the truth?*

At *this* more ultimate stage, or course, considerations of cognitive or theoretical rationality can no longer themselves be deployed successfully. To rely upon them in the defense of rationality is to move in a circle. The time is now at hand when one must go outside the whole cognitive/theoretical sphere. One clearly cannot marshal an ultimately adequate defense of rational cognition by an appeal that proceeds wholly on its own ground. It becomes necessary to seek a cognition-external rationale of justification, and now, at this final stage, the aforementioned pragmatic appeal to the conditions of effective action properly come into operation. Now the time is finally at hand for taking the pragmatic route.

The "ought" in "Men ought to be rational" is in the final analysis a *prudential* ought—and, as we saw in the last chapter, certainly not a *moral* ought. That is, one should be rational *if one is to be effective and efficient in the realization of one's chosen objectives* (whatever they may happen to be). The constraints to rationality are not those of *morality,* but those of *purposive efficacy.* Accordingly the rationale for subscribing to the established ground rules of probative procedure in inquiry ultimately lies in the domain of prudence and intelligent self-interest.[8]

This issue of the prudential and pragmatic justification of cognitive methodology has ramifications that need closer examination, above all, those relating to its developmental and evolutionary dimensions.[9]

8. Does this fact that rationality serves the interests of prudence mean that it is never rational to do something imprudent—something which, like an act of genuine altruism, puts one's self-interest at risk? Not at all. At bottom rationality is coordinate with an efficiency on purpose-attainment in general. And insofar as one's purposes are not self-regarding but relate to the welfare of other's regardless of one's own, rationality stands ready to facilitate these aims as well. (On the relationship of self-interested prudence and rationality, see the author's *Unselfishness* [Pittsburgh, 1975].)

9. The central theses of this chapter are developed more fully in the author's *Methodological Pragmatism* (Oxford, 1977).

7 Evolution-
ary episte-
mology and
the burden of
proof

1. The pragmatic-evolutionary justification of the standards of dialectical rationality

The foregoing pragmatic approach to cognitive justification has proceeded in the timeless present of theoretical validation. This is a serious shortcoming, for it overlooks the developmental and evolutionary aspect of the matter—an aspect that is in fact central for the legitimation of our cognitive instrumentalities.

Man is a relatively powerless creature emplaced *in medias res* in the difficult setting of a hostile or at best indifferent world. He can only survive (let alone thrive) by becoming not just a *rational*, but a *socially* rational animal. He must align his activities and undertakings with those of others for the cooperative realization of common interests. (Darwin himself stressed the evolutionary value to man of intelligent cooperation.) Life is short and the individual person by himself is powerless. This requirement of acting jointly with others for the common good establishes a need to coordinate the actions of people. Cooperative and concerted action—and therefore effective communication and persuasion—become crucial instruments of survival. Inquiry thus emerges as a social and communal process, and the probative ground rules by which we persuade one another are basic to the rational enterprise.

Our methodological approach to the dialectic process can accordingly be viewed in a historical or developmental perspective that displays it in a Hegelian light. Such a dialectical methodology of inquiry proceeds by way of a succession of opposed "moments" of thesis-critical testing and thesis-favoring support, of positive defense alternating with rationale-probing critiques. The cyclical form of the process at issue here was already set out in Chapter Three along the lines depicted in Figure 7. The dialectical process serves not only to improve on the articulation of our commitment on the side of its *content* but also to exhibit its rational *structure* of evidential interrelationships—to generate through one synoptic process both a refined articulation of the statement of a maintained thesis and its supportive framework of systematic grounding. The parallelism between "inquiry" as a temporal process of discovery in historic time and a logical process of justification in systematic exposition is striking and unmistakable. Indeed in extreme—or idealized—cases the structure of the two processes will coincide in isomorphic replication.

Figure 7
THE DIALECTIC OF INQUIRY

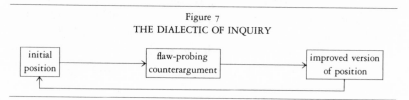

The cyclic process has important ramifications. Men are invariably and inevitably born into a preexisting world with a preexisting social order and a preexisting body of knowledge or purported knowledge. And so we always set out from a standard of presumption (and cognitive practice generally) that is already in place: we are never required to proceed *ex nihilo*. But, of course, these given standards are corrigible under the pressure of trial and error. (Both *formal* factors of systematic efficiency and elegance and *material* factors of practical efficacy and pragmatic success play a pivotal role in delimiting this range of "error.") Though we always start from a *given* position, the motivation for and prospect of improvements in the inquiry process is ever present. An evolutionary process of natural selection—or rather *rational* selection—is at work here. For a community of (generally) rational agents will tend to perpetuate—in its practice and in its teaching of oncoming generations—predominantly those methods and principles of procedure that prove themselves in the efficient production of desired results.

The ultimate justification of the established rational standards emerges in the light of these considerations as evolutionary in character. And "evolution" enters in two ways. For one thing, these standards conduce to *survival* (or, more generally, *goal-realization*) for us men, so that they play an instrumental role in *our* evolution by *natural* selection. Moreover they are themselves evolved, through an historic process of retaining what works and abandoning what doesn't, so that these standards themselves evolve through a process of *rational* selection. They are evolutionary instruments which themselves have an evolutionary history in which their legitimation resides.

It has long been recognized that evolutionary considerations preempt a contention of the type "Is it not wondrous to the point of miracle that man's sense organs (eyes, ears, etc.) are so elegantly attuned to the transactions of our physical environment as to be able to provide us with such useful data about it!" An analogous response is clearly in order with respect to the issue of accounting for the efficiency of our cognitive methodologies. One can counter by essentially analogous evolutionary moves any sceptical surprise at the claim that our cognitive procedures of probative inquiry and substantiating argumentation should be effective in providing us with useful information about the world. Accordingly the question "But why should we accept as (presumably) true the conclusions of 'good arguments' according to the standards that have established themselves in general currency?" can in the final analysis be anwered along evolutionary lines.

The justification of probative rationality (both on the side of what it *is* and what it *does*) is thus pragmatic and evolutionary—it is a matter of the confluence or consilience of pragmatic success with evolutionary survival through *rational* selection. The rationale of probative rationality is pragmatic—but with a markedly Darwinian twist.

To be sure, various writers have, from the very inception of epistemological Darwinism, argued against this line of approach. And the major criticisms of evolutionary theories of epistemic validation all have a common core and purport. All proceed by dwelling heavily on the distinction between the cognitive/intellectual side of human affairs and their affective/physical side. They insist that there is no decisive reason of theoretical principle why conceptions and beliefs conducive to the welfare of man should be cognitively valid.[1] After all, survival-conducive beliefs are surely not *invariably* (and perhaps not even *generally*) correct; nor need correct beliefs necessarily prove survival-conducive. This objection poses a serious difficulty for any program of evolutionary epistemology.

By way of a useful analogy, consider again J. S. Mill's contention (advanced in *On Liberty*) that the competition among schools of thought is akin to that between biological varieties: the rivalry among ideas for acceptance amounts to a struggle for existence (i.e., perpetuation or *continued existence*), a struggle in which those beliefs which are the fittest—viz., those that represent "the truth"—must finally prevail. The survival of beliefs within an intellectual community is viewed as parallel with biological survival.

It is perhaps unnecessary to dwell, at this stage, on the shortcomings of this unduly optimistic theory. Acceptance of theses is all too often governed by extrarational factors: mere entrenchment, faddism, social pressures, bandwagons, propaganda ("thought control"), etc. And there can be no secure assurance that such perturbations will inevitably or even usually be eliminated in the course of time.

The view that the inherent attractions of the truth assure its ultimate victory in a struggle for acceptance among the beliefs of imperfect humans thus seems overly hopeful. However, its most serious shortcomings stem from its operation at the *thesis* level. An evolutionary approach oriented towards the more general level of probative

---

1. The fundamentals of this line of thought go back to Plato's myth of the cave (in Bk. II of the *Republic*) with its moral that too close a heed of the realities and practicalities of this world will impede those unconstrained excursions of intellect through which alone an insight into theoretic truth can be obtained. Henri Bergson developed at length this theme that only by separating the mind from the restraints of quotidian action-directedness can man achieve a proper understanding of reality, as there is no reason to think that a cognitive apparatus which has evolved for *survival* purposes should provide a handle on *theoretical* truth. (See his *Essai sur les donnees immédiats de la conscience*, 8th ed. [Paris, 1889], as well as his *Introduction à la métaphysique* in the *Revue de la métaphysique et de morale*, vol. 2 [1903], pp. 1–183.) In recent days this position—that the aims of survival-promotion and knowledge-enhancement may even be antithetical—has been vigorously argued by Hermann Tennessen. (See his "Knowledge versus Survival," *Inquiry* 16 [1973] 407–414; and also "On Knowing What One Knows Not," in J. Royce and W. Rozeboom (eds.), *The Psychology of Knowing* [New York, 1972], pp. 111–160.)

methods seems to have substantially greater promise. The generality and open-endedness of a cognitive *methodology* furnish it with a capacity to wash out the influence of these fortuitous and extraneous factors. Such a methodology is so general and so open-ended in its orientation that gratuitous success on a *systematic* basis can be ruled out as a genuine prospect. The danger of adventitious or fortuitous efficacy is effectively removed where a *systematic* method of inquiry is concerned—a method which must by its very synoptic nature press deeply into the sphere of the pragmatically effective. The *methodological* turn of the present approach towards thesis-validating methods of inquiry thus becomes crucial here.

2. Hume's problem

At this point, however, the acute sceptic falls back on Hume. He asks:

> How can you be sure that the future will resemble the past? To be told of our cognitive methods that they have worked well in the past and have proven themselves as wonderfully adaptive simply invites the obvious question: what guarantee is there that these probative practices will continue to be comparably effective in the future?

We thus return finally—and perhaps fatally—to Hume's problem of the validation of reasoning from past to future.

To begin with, it is obvious that if one attempts any *experiential* justification of the acceptability-as-true criteriology C of a probative methodology of inquiry, then one obtains a line of argument whose direction of motion is as follows:

C has provided satisfactory results → C provides satisfactory
results in general

And such reasoning would comprise *a fortiori* the subargument whose principal direction of motion is as follows:

C has provided satisfactory results → C will provide satisfactory
results

This clearly encounters Humean difficulties. For it seems that what is at issue here is still an *argument,* though now one of the *practical* form:

works in the past→works in the future

rather than the theoretical/cognitive form:

true in the past→true in the future.

Appearances to the contrary notwithstanding, however, what is at issue here is *not* the establishment of a factual thesis—such as the regularity of nature—but the validation of a practice. For what matters here is a practical policy: to continue to employ a method that has proven to be successful (i.e., more effective than alternatives) in those cases (of suitable numerousness, variety, etc.) where it has been tried. The issue, accordingly, is not one of establishing a factual thesis but one of validating a practical course of action. And from this methodological perspective, the problem is not that of the question "How does one validate an *inference* from past-oriented premises to a future-oriented conclusion?" but that of the question "Why should a method's having *some* success count as evidence towards its efficacy more generally?" And the answer to this pivotal question lies in a fundamentally this-or-nothing argument:

> If you are prepared to let *anything* in the line of available information count as evidence for a practical precept of the ∅-works-in-general type (that is, if in this practical context you are going to play the rationality game of giving evidence and reasons at all), then you simply have no alternative to letting ∅-works-in-some-cases count, because it is true *as a matter of principle* that in the case of a practice, method, or procedure rooted in the contingent sphere of empirical fact this is the only sort of "evidence" of suitability that one can ever hope to have in hand.

3. Shifting the burden of proof against the sceptic

This methodological turn in fact manages to shift the burden of proof against the sceptic by a subtle maneuver.

To see how this is so, it is necessary, first of all, to pay heed once more to the ancient recognition of the essentially amphibious nature of man as a creature of intellect and will, of thought and action; a creature capable both of beliefs and deeds, of saying and doing. It thus becomes important to recognize the distinction between (1) the essentially *intellectual/theoretical* issue of having certain *beliefs* (viz., accepting that *P* is the case); (2) the essentially *practical* issue of espousing certain *actions* (viz., accepting that *X* is to be done), and (3) the complexedly Janus-faced issue of *methodology* (tools, procedures, policies, and rules for action, etc.) which looks both in theoretical and in practical directions.

As a *rational* being, man must certainly have some sort of adequate *rationale* for proceeding in all three of these cases: the beliefs he deems worthy of acceptance, the actions he deems worthy of performance, and the procedures he deems it proper to follow. And, of course, in all such cases the burden of proof goes against the proposer—in each instance there is an initiating burden of proof (I-burden) that goes against the item at issue. But when we consider the evidential burden of proof (E-burden), the matter stands rather differently in the different cases. For it is crucial here that established *theses* and established *methods stand on a quite different footing as regards their potential legitimation.*

The fact that a certain belief has generally been held with respect to some issue at best constitutes an item of very weak evidence in its favor. Unless further special aspects of the case are involved, the factor of general adoption provides a relatively feeble evidential basis for theses, one that can go only a very short distance in shifting the initial presumption and reallocating the burden of proof.[2] When it has been shown that a certain *belief* is generally accepted, it may still be plausibly maintained that—in view of the gullibility of men—the burden of proof yet pretty much remains against it. But when it has been shown that a certain *method* has come to be generally adopted the

---

2. Some may think this position too cautious. For a spirited defense of the evidential significance of general acceptance, see Daniel Goldstick, "Methodological Conservatism," *American Philosophical Quarterly* 8 (1971): 186–191. Goldstick argues the position that *"a priori* and in principle, it is possible (at least sometimes) to make out a good *prima facie* case for a proposition by citing the fact that it is' believed by us (*ibid.,* p. 186).

situation changes. General espousal of a method within a community of rational agents implies success in teaching its objectives, and success is everywhere a valid—indeed *the* valid—criterion of methodological appropriateness. It is clearly debatable whether or not an established *belief* deserves to have a presumption of truth conceded in its favor (the probative situation is unquestionably murky here). But there can be no real question that an established *method*—one which has "proven itself" over a wide variety of applications within its range of correlative objectives—has solid claims to a presumption in its favor.

To be sure, its experiential support through evidence-in-hand regarding its record of success does not *demonstrate* that a method will succeed in future applications. But the probative weight of experience cannot be altogether discounted: established success must be allowed to carry *some* weight. A tried and successful method has a presumption in its favor. For while established success is no *proof* of further efficacy, it does succeed in shifting the *burden* of proof in a favorable direction. In warranting a method there is no need for a prior demonstration of guaranteed efficacy. It suffices that the evidence— i.e., such evidence as we can actually hope to gather—shows that this method is as promising as any plausible alternative. The rationality of the practical domain is such that the requisites of method-use justification are less demanding than those of thesis-acceptance justification. And this general circumstance remains operative even in the cognitive sphere, where the methods at issue are methods for warranting the acceptance of theses.

There is no reason why even a perfectly rational inquirer acting cautiously on the best evidence at his disposal might not often trade in true theses for false ones, when this evidence simply points in the wrong direction. But it is a far-fetched and unrealistic prospect that a method of systematically superior performance-capabilities would ever be traded in for an inherently inferior one, given that the rational man adopts methods on the basis of their manifested superiority. And these *general* truths about methods apply to *cognitive* methods with particular force. Where a method of the range and many-sidedness of a probative methodology of inquiry is concerned, manifest superiority in performance is a well-nigh decisive indicator of *inherent* adequacy.

Given the ramifications and complexities of the cognitive enterprise, there is good reason to think that our presently available cognitive principles are produced by an evolutionary process that favor the fittest methods. And as a result it makes sense to construe actual currency as adequacy-indicative in this domain.

But why should systematic success in application or implementation be accepted as rationally justifying continued use of a method, when this would clearly not suffice to justify acceptance of any corresponding thesis? Why, in short, is the probative rationality of the *practical* realm more lenient than that of the *theoretical?*

The answer lies in the crucial difference between the domain of theory and that of praxis. Pure theory is never under any constraint to arrive at any resolution—by its very nature it operates in the absence of such pressures. Whenever the evidence seems somehow imperfect or insufficient, theory is free to suspend judgment and await fuller information. But in the sphere of action the case is rather different. For even "inaction" is a mode of action in this domain. And because we must act on the best available evidence—however imperfect it may be from some ideal point of view—the ground rules for rationally warranted action are bound to differ substantially from those which govern rational belief on the purely theoretical side. Thesis-acceptance requires very strong or conclusive evidence, if the requirements of rationality are to be met. But the circumstances of the practical sphere are such that relatively weak considerations on the side of attained success can serve to reverse the presumption against a method of proceeding. Just herein lies the advantage of the present two-tier approach which uses pragmatico-evolutionary considerations to legitimate a certain cognitive methodology (and not, be it noted, any substantive theses or hypotheses) and then validates particular theses in the standard way, by means of an established methodology of validation.

A pivotal factor of this pragmatically methodological approach to the critique of scepticism regarding matters of fact lies in the consideration that different facets of rationality come into play in different settings. In particular, the rationality of practice has (and *must* have) different ground rules from the rationality of theory, and the principles of presumption and burden of proof are bound to differ in the two contexts.

The critical point is that in the context of a justificatory argument with respect to methods and procedures one is *not* dealing with the establishment of a factual thesis at all—be it demonstrative or presumptive—but rather with the rational validation of a course of action. And the practical warrant that rationalizes the use of a method—even a method for the validation of knowledge-claims— need not call for a failproof guarantee of success (which is, in the circumstances of the case in view, altogether impossible), but merely for possession of reasons as good as we can expect under the circumstances. In the realm of action—unlike that of theory—the concept of rationality operates in a variant manner. For here the presumption in favor of established methods (but not theses!) tilts the burden of proof in this context against a sceptical opponent.

The difference between theses and methods is thus crucial for our present purposes. It provides the rationale for taking the fact that a method has worked in certain other cases as basis for its application in the present case (in the absence of any explicit counterindications). And this point regarding methods in general applies equally to our specifically *cognitive* methods. Here again, considerations of burden of proof operate in such a way as to blunt the cutting edge of the sceptic's all-too-destructive weapons.[3]

3. Further amplification of the evolutionary epistemology of this chapter can be found in the author's books on *The Primacy of Practice* (Oxford, 1973) and *Methodological Pragmatism* (Oxford, 1977).

8 The disputational model of scientific inquiry

1. The disputational approach

Our legitimation of the standard probative mechanisms of inquiry regarding factual matters began with the factor of pragmatic success and subsequently transmuted this into an issue of Darwinian survival. As the discussion has already foreshadowed at many points, it is clearly the *method of scientific inquiry* that has carried the day here. The mechanisms of scientific reasoning clearly represent the most developed and sophisticated of our probative methods. No elaborate argumentation is necessary to establish the all-too-evident fact that science has come out on top in the competition of rational selection with respect to alternative processes for the substantiation of factual claims. This line of thought lends a special interest to the question of the role of dialectical/disputational considerations within science itself.

This final chapter will explore the prospects of devising a disputational model for scientific inquiry. The basic idea of such a model is to cast the innovating scientist in the role of an *advocate* who sets out to propound and defend a certain thesis. Thus the scientist, viewed *ex officio* in the role of proponent, does not approach the study of nature as the "impartial" or "detached" or "indifferent" searcher of the traditional picture. He is—literally—a *proponent*, one who is concerned to maintain a thesis and seeks to build the best case for it that he possibly can. Rather than being an indifferent searcher, he is a committed and partisan exponent of a particular thesis or point of view.

At this stage, however, the social or communal aspect of the scientific enterprise comes crucially into play. For once a scientifically significant thesis is propounded by someone, the "scientific community" provides (1) certain *opponents,* in the form of self-appointed critics who challenge this thesis in an adversary manner, probing for its weak points and seeking to impede its acceptance, and (2) a larger, neutral body of concerned but otherwise uncommitted bystanders, who effectively act as *arbiters* of the "dispute." From this perspective, creative science appears in the light of an *adversary procedure,* with proponents and opponents carrying on a debate to secure the approbation of knowledgeable but "disinterested" (i.e., unaligned) parties—often as not the rising generation of specialists in the field.[1]

Such a process clearly exhibits the traditional structure of a disputation: the proponent scientist advances a thesis and seeks to develop a case for its acceptance; his opponents try to knock it down; the arbiter looks on from the sidelines to effect an eventual adjudication. And, of course, the burden of proof rests, as always, with the proponent. His is the task of bringing forward evidence and supporting his thesis against objections.

The proponent of a scientific thesis thus endeavors to build up for it a solid evidential case; his opponents endeavor to block this case by seeking out discordant considerations. The probative rules of the game here are supplied by the usual accounts of scientific methodology in terms of "inductive logic," the design of experiments, the statistical organon of evidential inquiry, and so on. And, of course, in the background looms the machinery of disputational "termination," the ultimate standards of assessment, the traditional trinity of the purposive teleology of science: explanatory adequacy, predictive success, and efficacious control vis-à-vis the world about us.

Accordingly, in scientific dialectic, as elsewhere, the probative ground rules play a pivotal role. This is not the place for a discourse on scientific method, and so virtually telegraphic brevity will have to suffice in indicating the evidential factors in support of the theoretical hypotheses that constitute scientific theses, viz., (1) their ability to serve as bases for successful predictions and applications (to facilitate "control over nature"), and (2) their systematic coherence with other-

---

1. Recall here Max Planck's oft-cited statement: "A new scientific truth is not usually presented in a way that convinces its opponents . . . ; rather they gradually die off, and a rising generation is familiarized with the truth from the start." (*Wissenschaftliche Selbstbiographie* [Leipzig, 1948], p. 22.)

wise accepted facts or purported facts, and above all (3) their capacity to facilitate the efficient explanatory systematization of such facts (subject to such principles as simplicity, uniformity, etc.).

Such an approach to scientific inquiry by no means denies the crucially important role of the standard considerations regarding the nature of scientific evidence as considered in the theory of the design of experiments, the study of scientific methodology, the theory of "inductive logic," etc. For on a disputational model, the normative rules of argumentation and evidence are clearly needed to function in their usual role as guideposts for the probative routing of the course of argumentation. The dialectical model does not dismiss the standard evidential considerations or deny them the pivotal force that is their due. Quite to the contrary, these now appear as playing a pivotal role—but one that is played out *within* the framework of the dialectical process. They furnish an indispensable component of the probative machinery essential to any dialectical approach to inquiry. The dialectical model of scientific inquiry does not come to destroy the rational mechanisms of the inductive methodology in science, but to fulfill them.[2]

Experimentation plays a central role in this probative process. The devising of experiments to probe a theory at its weakest points, experiments which might—if their eventuation is suitably negative—throw serious doubt upon its claims, comes to be an objective that proponent and opponent share in common. This is so because *counterindicative* experimental findings are a powerful, indeed virtually decisive weapon in the opponent's armory. And on the other hand, the *favorable* issue of such an experimental test is a strong asset to the

2. Aristotle's position is particularly interesting in this connection. His view of scientific systematization is rigidly deductive and "Euclidean" in its orientation. But the search for the middle term of a scientifically demonstrative syllogism in actual inquiry is the key task, and dialectic affords a most efficient means towards its realization. (In this sense the *Topics* can be looked upon as a methodological supplement to the theory of *epistēmē* put forward in *Posterior Analytics*.) Aristotle's general approach was refined by St. Thomas Aquinas and is still current, *mutatis mutandis*, among contemporary Thomists, who perhaps comprise the largest single current "school" to espouse a dialectical view of scientific method. The best modern expositor of the position is Charles de Koninck whose views are surveyed in Ralph McInerny, "Charles de Koninck: A Philosopher of Order," The New Scholasticism 39 (1965): 691–516. A survey of this area is given in Paul R. Durbin, O. P., *Logic and Scientific Inquiry* (Milwaukee, 1968); see especially pp. 40–41, 67.

proponent's case. Even more than the capacity of his thesis to explain observational findings and to accommodate facts which appear anomalous from the standpoint of rival theories, the survival of his theory/thesis in the face of deliberate attempts at experimental invalidation is potent evidence for his case. Evidence of this sort reverses the E-burden of proof, placing it upon the shoulders of the adversary. Accordingly, progress in natural science can be viewed as in substantial measure a matter of a dialogue or dialectical exchange between theoreticians and experimentalists, exchanges which themselves form part of a wider group of disputations between rival theorists.

Such a dialectical-disputational model of the process of scientific inquiry has many attractive features in accounting for the actual phenomenology of scientific work. Not only does it explain the element of competition that all too plainly characterizes the actual *modus operandi* of the scientific community.[3] It accounts also for the "Planck phenomenon" (of note 1 above), which envisages an old school of stubborn resistance to scientific innovation that is never conquered in the course of progress but simply bypassed.

2. Presumptions in science

Philosophers of science have frequently been exercised by the prominent but yet problematic role in science of such theoretical factors of inductive reasoning as *continuity, uniformity, regularity, conservation,* and *simplicity.* These are of particular interest from our present point of view. They are generally approached from one of two directions. Sometimes they are regarded as objective tendencies of nature—constitutive facts regarding a world whose mode of functioning exhibits not the *horror vacui* of the medievals but an analogous principle like *amor simplicitatis,* etc. On the other hand, they are sometimes cast in the role of principles whose weight bears wholly on the *subjects* who do scientific theorizing rather than in the *object* of their theories; they

---

3. Already over a century ago, William Whewell (in his *Novum Organon Renovatium* [London, 1858; Bk. II, Chap. II, sect. i, art. 2 and Bk. III, Chap. V]) cast controversy and discussion in the role of a crucial instrument for the elucidation of scientific ideas.

are held simply to reflect the subjective intellectual predilection of the working scientist rather than any objective features of the natural universe itself. But in fact neither side of this subjective/objective dichotomy is appropriate. For all these various facets of systematicity are most advantageously seen as principles of an essentially epistemological, or rather *methodological,* character. They represent *regulative* principles for the construction of *adequate* explanatory accounts.

Accordingly, it would be an ill-advised and wholly unnecessary complication to regard such principles as representing fundamentally *ontological* factors, as indicating a straightforward fact about the world—an inclination on the part of nature itself towards certain principles of operation (to put it somewhat anthropomorphically). It is best to view these principles as a (duly warranted) regulative or procedural or methodological facet of explanatory accounts, rather than a constitutive or descriptive (world-oriented) facet of nature. The probative methodology of scientific inquiry requires principles of this sort as part of the evaluative machinery of its own *modus operandi.* One should thus avoid treating such factors as the *results* of an inquiry for which they must in fact serve as *inputs.* They represent not so much substantive findings about nature as procedural, regulative ground rules for the conduct of scientific inquiry—procedural principles of plausibility that afford evaluative standards governing the provision of explanatory accounts.[4] (Just this view of, specifically, the *uniformity* of nature has been advanced by several recent writers.[5])

We have seen how disputation hinges on certain characteristic initial assessments of presumption and plausibility. Just what is the natural basis for these assessments in the domain of contingent fact? The

4. Compare T. S. Kuhn's statement that: "nature is vastly too complex to be explored even approximately at random. Something must tell the scientist where to look and what to look for." ("The Function of Dogma in Scientific Research," in B. A. Brody [ed.], *Readings in the Philosophy of Science* [Englewood Cliffs, 1970], pp. 356–373 [see p. 367].) The Kuhnian *paradigms* provide, for him, the main source of such presumptions. Most writers on the subject simply invoke *analogy.* See, for example, the interesting cases treated in G. Polya, *Induction and Analogy in Mathematics* (Princeton, 1954). The point at issue goes back at least to C. S. Peirce.

5. Cf. Stephen Toulmin, *The Philosophy of Science* (London, 1953), see especially sect. 5.2 "Physicists Work on Presumptions, Not Assumptions," pp. 144–148; and J. P. Day, "The Uniformity of Nature," *American Philosophical Quarterly* 12 (1975). Compare also the author's essay "On the Self-Consistency of Nature," in *The Primacy of Practice* (Oxford, 1973), pp. 88–106.

answer to this crucial question of the standards of plausibility and presumption is simply that these standards are provided by the very conception of scientific systematicity itself. A positive presumption of acceptability is therefore to operate in favor of all the traditional parameters of systematization: consistency, uniformity, regularity (causality; rulishness and lawfulness in all forms), simplicity, connectedness/coherence, unity/compeleteness, etc. These are now to function as regulative presumptions—as principles of epistemic preferability. This is readily exemplified in cases of circumstances of attuning theory and data in curve fitting:

⌇⌇	not ⌇⌇	(simplicity)
⌇	not ⟋	(uniformity)
⌐	not ⟋	(cohesion)
—	not — —	(completeness)

Systematicity thus come to do double duty as a general criterion of acceptability-as-true and as a regulative principle of plausibility and presumption. The principles of systematicity now represent *presumptive principles regulatively governing the conduct of inquiry.*

This regulative standing of such parameters as principles of epistemic preferability is reflected in the schema:

> Other things being (anything like) equal, give precedence in acceptance-deliberations to those alternatives that in the context of other actual or putative commitments are relatively more uniform (or coherent or simple or complete, etc.) than their alternatives.

Our disputational approach to inquiry thus casts the basic parameters of systematicity as regulative principles of plausibility and preference, transforming them from *adequacy principles of system structure* to *selection principles for system inclusion.* Their crucial features from this perspective are:

1. They are *regulative,* that is, they guide our cognitive actions by telling us how to proceed in system design. ("Of alternative accounts, *adopt* the most simple, uniform, etc.")
2. They are *preferential,* that is, they guide the issue of cognitive precedence and priority. ("Of alternative accounts, give precedence, priority, preference to the most simple, uniform, etc.")

3. They are *essentially negative,* that is, like the Old Testament rules implicit in the injunctions of the *Pentateuch,* they are to be construed negatively in terms of *avoid!, shun!, minimize!* with respect to such factors as complexity, disuniformity, etc.

The crucial consideration for our present purposes is that the role in scientific reasoning of factors like continuity, simplicity, uniformity, and all the other cognitive desiderata embraced within the ambit of inductive systematization, could be rationalized quite adequately from the perspective of probative methodology, and specifically considerations of burden of proof—that is, by regarding them in the light of *presumptions.* These factors accordingly regulate the sorts of suppositions that it is reasonable to make in the absence of any explicit indications to the contrary. Their role is that of presumptions which are "in possession of the field" as the scientist goes about the work of constructing explanatory accounts regarding the phenomena of nature. They stand at any rate until such time as they are explicitly displaced by counterevidence.

This perspective from the angle of probative methodology—viewing the principles of the uniformity of nature, the regularity of nature, etc., as forming a standard part of the probative machinery, and so implementing the usual mechanisms of plausibility and presumption—obviously dovetails well with the present disputational view of scientific inquiry. All of these familiar methodological principles of science will, in the present approach, figure among the presumptions operative within the probative ground rules governing the dialectic of scientific argumentation.[6]

3. The probative significance of the history of science

It is worth digressing briefly on one interesting aspect of the dialectical approach to science, namely the special importance with which

---

6. For a fuller discussion of plausibility and presumption, see the author's *Plausible Reasoning* (Assen, 1976).

it endows the *history* of science, even in a concern simply for the seemingly ahistorical, purely systematic issue of the "truth of the matter."

In our earlier discussion of the nature of the /-relationship of probative grounding we saw that this concerns the giving of good reasons in a way that falls short of conclusive evidence. As a consequence, it emerged that *detachment* is not possible, so that we cannot reason

$$\frac{P/Q}{\begin{array}{c} Q \\ \hline \therefore P \end{array}}$$

That is, once P/Q and Q are given, we cannot simply forget about them, proceeding to "detach" P and henceforth to let this thesis stand by itself, in splendid isolation from its probative background. The /-relationship is such that P/Q means if Q then "other things being equal" also P and this means we must always look to "the other things"—that the configuration of surrounding information always remains a crucial consideration because not only the *content* of the evidence but the entire *course of argumentation* by which it is marshalled plays a key role. In a dialectical setting we can evaluate the probative standing of a thesis only in its concrete context—against the background complex of plausibilities and presumptions that underpin it within the specific course of argumentation by which this thesis is supported.

To assess the solidity (i.e., *validity*) of a *deductive* argument, we must simply determine that the conclusion is such that IF the premisses are true, THEN it must be true as well. The *way* in which the conclusion is linked to the premisses—the actual course of argumentation itself—is ultimately irrelevant. In deductive arguments, a thesis can shed its probative antecedents: if it is established relative to established theses it becomes established *per se*—the element of relativity or contextuality disappears.

But with a *nondeductive* argument—and a dialectical argument in particular—the situation is very different. In a dialectical setting the epistemic standing of the conclusion always remains a *relative* status—one relativized to the line of argumentation at issue. Here a close scrutiny of the actual course of argumentation is an indispensable part of the assessment of probative solidity. We can determine the probative status of the thesis only "in context"—only relative to the historical concreta' of its probative background. Its status relative to a course of argument hinges on its antecedents within this argument in such a way that these cannot be put aside: it becomes important to consider not just the *content* of the evidence, but also the *historical development* of the evidential situation. The whole course of argumentation must be brought into the assessment of the probative status of the conclusion.

These general considerations regarding the probative structure of dialectical contexts have one particularly significant bearing in the specific setting of a disputational model of natural science. They mean that we can never really assess the probative standing of a scientific thesis outside its historical context—outside the background of the actual course of controversy and discussion from which it has emerged. The real-life sequence of argumentation and debate that has brought us to where we are becomes a crucial factor in the rational assessment of this position. The probative or evidential situation in this domain is context-dependent on the details of the historical background in a way that finds no parallel in the deductive sciences that have often (and mistakenly) been taken as the model of scientific rationality in general.

These considerations go very much against the grain of the positivist philosophy of science. Here Hans Reichenbach's well-known distinction between the "context of discovery" and the "context of justification" reigned supreme.[7] The position is that the historical considerations regarding the discovery or generation of a hypothesis is wholly irrelevant to the issue of its testing and evolution. Discovery relates to the *psychology* of science, justification to its *logic,* and never the twain need meet. As Reichenbach insists: "Epistemology does not regard the processes of thinking in their actual occurrence. . . ."[8] Our present position goes against the grain of this view, arguing (on

7. Hans Reichenbach, *The Rise of Scientific Philosophy* (Berkeley and Los Angeles, 1951). Compare Karl R. Popper, *The Logic of Scientific Discovery* (New York, 1959) and Carl G. Hempel, "Recent Problems of Induction" in R. G. Colodny (ed.), *Mind and Cosmos* (Pittsburgh, 1966).

8. *The Rise of Scientific Philosophy*, p. 5.

roughly evolutionary grounds) that *some* issues of historical development are bound to be probatively significant.

But consider the following objection:

> This approach commits the *genetic fallacy:* it imports considerations of the course of development and the historical background and antecedents of contentions into the question of probative justification. (As, for example, when one argues from the fact that a doctrine had a somehow reputable [or disreputable] origin that it must be tenable [or untenable].) In short, it confuses historical and justificatory considerations. But this is improper. One cannot move from the historical order of temporal development to the evidential order of probative concatenation.[9]

The response here is simply that two very different ranges of reasoning are at issue. The "genetic fallacy" is indeed objectionable within the setting of the *deductive* framework of reasoning. But in *dialectical* situations—where the issue of probative force depends not just on the *content* of the supportive considerations but also (in the absence of a "law of detachment") upon the actual historical structure of their course of development, there is no fallacy in the heed of genetic considerations. No one expects an inductive argument to be deductively valid. Even so, one should not expect what is deductively fallacious to be dialectically fallacious as well.

4. Confirmationism vs. falsificationism

The field of scientific epistemology is currently the battleground between two major rival schools of thought. On the one hand, we find the *confirmationists* who, following Carnap, insist on the primacy of the search for *confirming evidence* for scientific hypotheses. They cast the scientist in the role of a collector who accumulates the evidence in favor of his theoretical hypotheses. From this perspective *the search for confirming evidence* is the prime task of science. On the other hand, we find the *falsificationists* who, following Popper, stress the importance

9. For the "genetic fallacy," see M. R. Cohen and E. Nagel, *An Introduction to Logic and Scientific Method* (New York, 1934), pp. 388–390. The fallaciousness at issue is already argued in Bernard Bosanquet, *Logic*, vol. II, 2nd ed. (Oxford, 1911), pp. 243ff.

of vulnerability to *experimental invalidation* and insist on the primacy in science of devising critical tests for scientific hypotheses. The scientist, in such an approach, is not an evidence collector but a cognitive demolition expert.

The position of each school encounters serious difficulties and limitations in accounting for the process of scientific inquiry as actually conducted.

The confirmationist position offers no doctrine-internal basis for understanding why the scientist should be *daring*. Nothing within the boundaries set by framework of the theory itself provides a reason why the scientist should not simply limit himself to those very safe, if nearly trivial, hypotheses of whose confirmation he can be reasonably sure from the very outset. Confirmationism offers no rationale for the preoccupation of the working scientist with those theoretical conjectures which, given the information in hand, seem *interesting* in that they move in significant ways beyond our existing picture of how things work in the world.

On the other hand, the falsificationist position offers no doctrine-internal basis for understanding why the scientist should be *sensible*, why he should not indulge endlessly in grappling with utterly far-fetched (though not as yet falsified) hypotheses, spending all his time in the experimental test—and refutation—of the most wild and fanciful conjectures. The falsificationist position offers no account for the preoccupation of the working scientist with those theoretical conjectures which, given the information at hand, would seem "reasonable" or "plausible" (in that they are more or less consonant with what otherwise belongs to our general view of the way in which things work in the world).

Thus what is lacking from each of these doctrines in separation is an account of the full complexity of the scientific venture. Each seems one-sided in conveying only a part of the picture, for each seems to have a valid insight that it stresses to the exclusion of the no less valid insight of its rival.

The significant merit of the disputational model of scientific inquiry is its capacity to put these two seemingly discordant pieces together, combining them in a systematic harmony. The disputational model is able to effect this synthesis because it views scientific inquiry as a fundamentally social or communal enterprise—i.e., a dispute between rival parties before a neutral arbiter. This communal aspect of the scientific inquiry as a process of social endeavor is crucial for present purposes. And it is altogether lacking with the orthodox confirmationist and falsificationist theories. There is, of course, no reason whatever why a strictly isolated inquirer cannot set out to formulate theories and endeavor to confirm them or to project conjectures and endeavor to disconfirm them. Neither confirmationism nor falsificationism has any inherently social tendencies. The aspect of a process of interpersonal interaction is altogether lacking from these two doctrines.[10]

Now it is precisely its view of the scientific enterprise as a certain sort of social-interaction process—namely, as a disputation or debate—that enables the disputational model of scientific inquiry to overcome the indicated shortcomings of confirmationism and falsificationism. Let us consider in detail how this is so.

To begin with, the disputational model patently accommodates *both* the confirmationist *and* the falsificationist aspects of the science. The innovative scientist, in his role of proponent, has the corresponding task of building up a case, of marshalling the supportive evidence for his thesis. The burden of proof lies against any proposed theory, and this burden must be reversed by adducing the supporting data needed to build up a *prima facie* case. Here is the rationale of the confirmationist aspect of the situation and the ground for the scientist's search for confirming evidence (over and above failed falsifications). On the other hand, his gainsaying opponent wants to challenge his thesis and to undermine or refute his case. Here is the groundwork of the falsificationist aspect. Confirmationism (i.e., the accumulation of supportive evidence for a scientific thesis) and falsificationism (i.e., the attempted refutation of scientific conjectures) are thus both seen as correlative aspects of a common whole.

The disputational model thus brings confirmationism and falsifica-

10. No recent philosopher of science has propounded a disputational or dialectical model of the overall process of scientific inquiry that is explicitly social in its bearing. But a Popperian falsificationism unquestionably invites something of an adversary attitude towards scientific claims, though the disputational aspect of this adversary relationship never figures in Popper's own discussions. Perhaps Paul Feyerabend's branch of neo-Popperianism best lends itself to development in this general direction.

tionism together in a sort of Hegelian "higher synthesis." Both are seen as phases or stages (i.e., Hegelian "moments") within the uniting framework of the overall dialectical process.

But a pivotal problem yet remains untouched. How can one account for the peculiar mixture of *speculative daring* with *plausibilistic caution* that characterizes scientific innovation?

The crucial aspect of the debate or disputation at issue is that it is *wholly spontaneous:* it is not *arranged* like a medieval academic exercise or a scheduled debate between competing collegiate teams. Thus if he is to enter into the activity at all—if he is to "play the game"—the proponent of a scientific thesis must, as it were, recruit his own opponents and enlist the arbiters as well.

These considerations suggest the proper account of the characteristic mixture of speculative daring with plausibilistic caution. For unless his thesis is "challenging," unless it is creatively innovative in some essential respect, it will drop unheeded from the pen. A gauntlet is flung down that it is not worthwhile to pick up; an invitation is issued to a debate no one bothers to attend. The disputational process is simply aborted. To gain entry into the ongoing hubub of scientific discussion the proponent must be daring because otherwise his thesis lacks interest: failing to be sufficiently "disputable," it is impotent to gain a hearing.

But, of course, daring and disputability are only one side of the coin. To "play the game" is also to strive to *win*—and so not just to *enter into* a dispute, but to do so with some chance of prevailing, by bringing into realization the essential conditions of a successful "determination." And since these conditions of success are articulated in terms of the evidential merits of the overall case that can be developed, this accounts for the verificationist's insistence upon plausibility, security, and evidential caution.

The rationale of progress in science can thus be viewed as the product of a dialectical tension between two essentially opposed considerations: the *daring* in thesis-projection that is needed to launch an active dispute on its way and the caution of *evidential anchoring* needed for a reasonable prospect of success in the framework of such a debate. If—as with the rival verificationist and falsificationist doctrines—one of these elements is overstressed to the point of usurping the place of the other, a one-sidedly distorted and thus mistaken picture results. For insofar as our present analysis has any merit, the overall structure of the conduct of scientific inquiry is to be seen as *an adversary-proceeding that conforms to the pattern of a dialectical process modeled on disputation*. And the circumstances under which such a disputation is carried on are such that a judicious mixing of daring and caution is essential to the enterprise.

5. The communal aspect

This disputational model indicates and emphasizes the fundamentally communal aspect of scientific work. Inquiry in science is seen as a process of interpersonal interaction involving proponents, opponents, and detached arbiters. Science accordingly appears as an enterprise with a characteristically social structure of its own.

The social and communal aspect of science has, of course, been stressed by many commentators. The novelty of the present approach pertains solely to its specific form. For the usual picture is that science is communal because it is a *collaborative and cooperative* enterprise subject to the desirability of a division of labor and the gain of efficiency by means of specialization. From this aspect, disagreements, the clash of conflicting schools of thought, and the conflicts of rival camps are seen as uniformly regrettable phenomena. They are viewed as divisive abberations, due to the unfortunate weaknesses of human nature (selfishness, pride, peevishness, and the like), and are thus taken to reflect a lamentable dissension in the ranks of science which retards the smooth progress of the enterprise.

If the theory proposed here is even partially correct, this traditional view—against which much recent philosophy of science from Polyani to Toulmin and Kuhn has been in rebellion—does indeed require drastic revision. For insofar as a disputational model of the scientific enterprise in terms of a dialectical adversary procedure has any merit, it is clear that a very different stance towards conflict and controversy is called for. For it now comes to be a mark not of malignancy but of health that competing schools of thought should endeavor to argue for conflicting theories by the most powerfully supportive reasonings they can marshal. Rivalry, competition, and conflict must now be seen not as unhappy aberrations, as deviant and regrettable manifestations of a human perversity that impedes the smooth progress of science; rather, they become a natural and requisite component of the ongoing process of scientific advance.[11]

In providing a plausible explanatory basis for such a controversy-oriented analysis of scientific work—one which certainly reflects the empirical realities far better than its cooperation-oriented rivals—the disputational approach can render a useful service to the theory of knowledge. And this upshot is the critically important aspect of the present discussion. For it is a guiding objective throughout this book to expound a version of "dialectic" that does not put the dialectical enterprise into opposition with science, but sees the dialectical and the scientific approaches to rationality as mutually complementary aspects of one unified cognitive endeavor.[12]

11. It is too obvious to need much elaboration that the disputational model of scientific inquiry will have very significant implications for the historiography of science, not only in giving a wholly new weight to false starts and efforts expended in ultimately fruitless directions, but also in serving as a heuristic guide to the explanation of just why scientific innovators have argued as they have in reacting to certain types of opposition.

12. The use of dialectics as an instrument for specifically *philosophical* inquiry goes beyond the limits of the present discussion. This has been the theme of an active revival by a "Chicago School" of philosophers. See Mortimer Adler, *Dialectic* (New York, 1927); Richard McKeon, *Freedom and History: The Semantics of Philosophical Controversies and Ideological Conflicts* (New York, 1952); Otto Bird, "Dialectic in Philosophical Inquiry," *Dialectica* 9 (1955): 287–304.

Name Index

Acton, H. B., 70n
Adler, Mortimer, 124n
Albert, Hans, 55n
Anderson, A. R., 64n, 71&n
Aquinas, St. Thomas, 112n
Aristotle, xi, 2, 18n, 23n, 39n, 41n, 58n, 112n
Asenjo, F. G., 71&n
Ayer, A. J., 93&n

Belnap, Nuel, 64n, 71&n
Bergson, Henri, 103n
Berkeley, George, 52
Bird, Otto, 124n
Blakely, T. J., 70n
Bochenski, I. M., 61n, 70n
Bosanquet, Bernard, 119n
Brentano, Franz, 34
Burke, Kenneth, xi(n)

Caney, David, 70n
Carnap, Rudolf, 82n, 119
Carneades, 37n, 94n
Castaneda, Hector-Neri, 72n
Chance, Janet, 80&n
Chisholm, R. M., 34, 72n, 79&n
Church, Alonzo, 61n, 70n
Cicero, 2&n
Clifford, W. K., 79-81
Cohen, M. R., 119n
Costello, W. T., 3n

Da Costa, Newton, 71&n
Day, J. P., 114n
Descartes, René, 34, 35&n, 58
Doz, André, 71n
Dubarle, Dominique, 71n
Durbin, Paul, 112n
Dürr, Karl, 52n

Engels, Friedrich, 69-70
Epstein, Richard, 26n, 29n, 31n, 32n
Evans, J. D. G., xi(n)

Feyerabend, Paul, 121n
Findlay, J. N., 72n
Freeley, A. J., 2n
Fulda, Hans xi(n)

Garfinkel, Harold, 33n
Gilby, Thomas, 2n, 8n
Goddard, Leonard, 72n
Goldstick, Daniel, 106n
Gonseth, Ferdinand, 40n

Hänggi, Jürg, 69n
Hanson, Norwood, 40n
Hegel, G. W. F., xi, 46, 52n, 61, 69, 70&n
Hempel, C. G., 118n
Hogan, James, xi(n)
Horn, Ewald, 3n
Hume, David, 52, 94, 104
Hurwitz, Adolf, 3n

Ilbert, Sir Courtenay, 26n, 27n, 31n

James, William, 79-81, 94
Jaskowski, Stanislaw, 62n, 71&n

Kamlah, Wilhelm, 73n
Kant, Immanuel, xi(n)
Kauber, Peter, 79&n
Kaufmann, Georg, 3n
Kline, G. L., 61n, 70n
de Koninck, Charles, 112n
Kosok, Michael, 70n
Kuhn, T. S., 114n, 123
Küng, Guido, 72n

125

Subject Index

127

SUBJECT INDEX

Marxist dialectics, 69-70
methodological turn, 95-99, 106-109

normality, 40

onus probandi, 2-3, 17, 25-45, 105-109
opponent(s), 2, 4, 111

plausibility, 37-41
pragmatism, 97-99
praxis, 93-95
presumption(s), 2-3, 7-8, 28-45, 113-116
probative asymmetries, 17-18
probative rationality, 75-82
proof, burden of, 2-3, 17, 25-45, 105-109
proponent, 2, 4, 110
provisoed assertion, 6-8
provisoed counterassertion, 10-11
provisoed denial, 9

rational acceptance, 75-82
rational inquiry, 46-60, 53-60
rationality, 84-88, 94-95

rationality, probative, 75-82
regulative principles in science, 115-116
rule of detachment, 117
rules of language, 92-93

Scots verdict, 26
scepticism, cognitive, 83-99, 105-109
science as an adversary procedure, 111-113
science, history of, 116-119
science, regulative principles in, 115-116
scientific inquiry, disputational model of, 110-124
selfcontradiction, 62-63
simplicity, 39-40, 114-115
strong distinction, 12
strong exception, 12
syllogistic, 13-14
symbolic logic, "dialectical", 71

termination, 43-45

weak distinction, 12
weak exception, 12
written exposition, 52-53